CONTENTS

T0016508

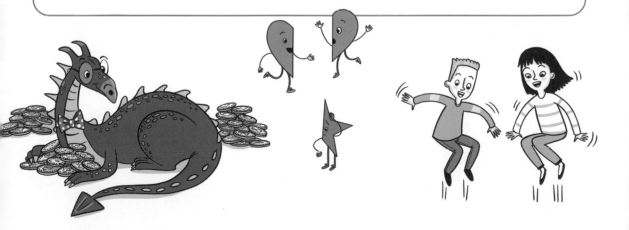

INTRODUCTION

Welcome to a book stuffed with mathematical mind-benders, challenges, activities, games to play, and things to make and do. But before we start ... what's it all about?

Making it count

As you know, mathematics is a school subject, and it's also studied by mathematicians—experts who spend their lives cracking brain-boggling number problems.

But there's much more to mathematics than that!

We have to learn about it in school for a good reason—it's a huge part of everyday life. You need numbers all the time, whether you're ...

Planning a time to meet your friends

Trying to find your way in a new place

Following a recipe to make dinner

Building something, from a model to a house

Figuring out how much money you can spend

Checking your temperature when you feel sick

... all kinds of things!

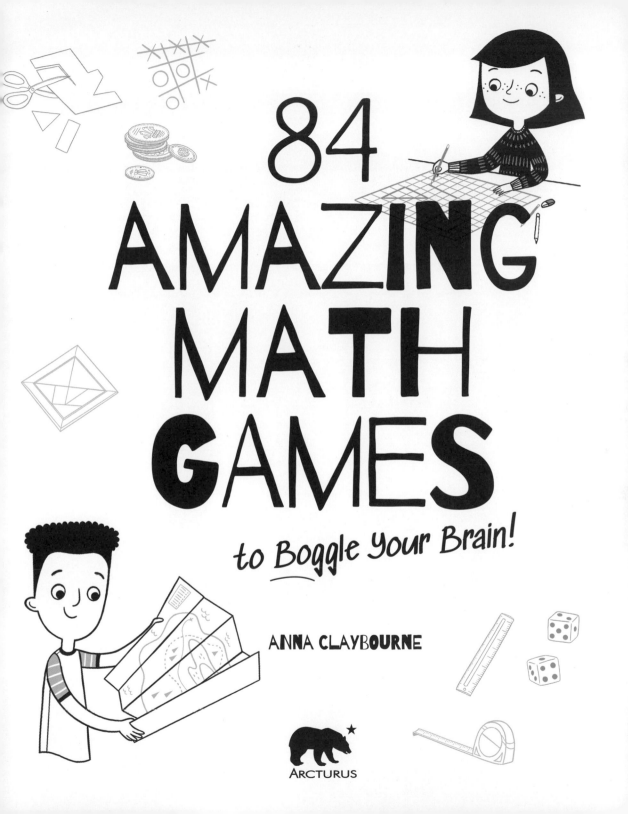

84 AMAZING MATH GAMES

to Boggle Your Brain!

ANNA CLAYBOURNE

ARCTURUS

This edition published in 2022 by Arcturus Publishing Limited
26/27 Bickels Yard, 151–153 Bermondsey Street,
London SE1 3HA

Author: Anna Claybourne
Illustrator: Amy Willcox
Editor: Susie Rae
Designer: Jeni Child
Design Manager: Jessica Holliland
Editorial Manager: Joe Harris

ISBN: 978-1-3988-1527-8
CH010105NT
Supplier 29, Date 0622, PI 00002119

Printed in China

What is STEM?

STEM is a worldwide initiative that
aims to cultivate an interest in
Science, Technology, Engineering, and
Mathematics, in an effort to promote
these disciplines to as wide a variety
of students as possible.

A world of numbers

Mathematics is a key part of science and technology. We need it to make things work—from making airplanes and rockets fly, to creating weather forecasts, to building skyscrapers and bridges that won't fall down, to making sure people take exactly the right amount of medicine.

If we didn't do the mathematics to get all these things right, it would be a disaster!

Up, up, and away!

Have fun!

Mathematics isn't just important—it can also be fun. And you can make it extra fun by playing number, shape, and calculation games, like the ones in this book.

How does it work?

"Game Science" features that explain the big ideas behind the fun

We've got ...

Games you can play with just a piece of paper and a pencil

Games to keep you busy on a long trip

Group games to play at a party, with your class at school, or with a bunch of friends

Games to play on your own, two-player games, and multiplayer games

Ready to play? Step this way.

NIM

The games in this chapter are designed for two players.
Many of them have been played for hundreds or thousands of years.
Let's start with a classic—the game of Nim!

How to play

 Set up the game by arranging your pieces in four rows, like this:

What do you need?

- A flat surface
- 16 matching or similar objects—coins, counters, marbles, candy, or whatever you like

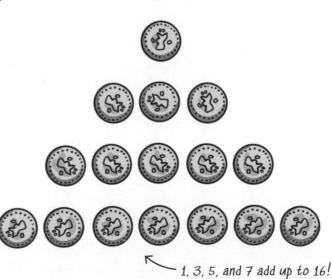

← 1, 3, 5, and 7 add up to 16!

6

Remember, you can't pick up coins from more than one row in one turn!

2 Now the players take turns picking up one or more pieces from the same row. You can take as many as you like, but they must all be from the same row.

3 The aim is to be the person who takes the last piece. That's all there is to it!

Game science

Mathematicians have spent ages studying how Nim works. When you play it a few times, you'll start to realize there are sneaky ways to make your opponent do what you want.

Try this, too!

There are many different variations of Nim. It can be played with different numbers of pieces and rows. For example, try playing with 12 pieces in three rows, like this.

You can also flip it around, so that the person who takes the last piece is the loser, not the winner.

HEX

To play the fantastic game of Hex, you need a special board made up of hexagons.

Set it up

1 Hex is usually played on a diamond-shaped board with 11 hexagons along each side. Two opposite sides are one shade, and the other two are another shade. It looks like this:

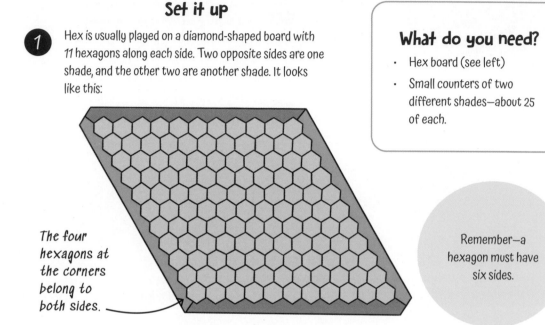

The four hexagons at the corners belong to both sides.

What do you need?

- Hex board (see left)
- Small counters of two different shades—about 25 of each.

Remember—a hexagon must have six sides.

2 You can copy this to make your own Hex board on a piece of cardboard, or if you have a computer and printer, you can find a blank Hex board online and print it out.

Just cut more if you run out!

3 You also need lots of small counters in the same two shades that will fit on the spaces. Use plastic counters if you have any, or cut small counters out of cardboard (about 25 of each).

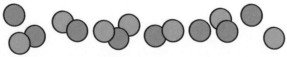

How to play

4 To play, the players pick a shade, then sit at the side of the board that matches their counters.

5 Then the two players take turns placing one of their counters anywhere on the board. Each player's aim is to make a chain of their counters all the way across the board, linking the two sides that match their chosen shade.

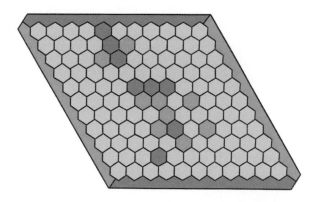

Game science

Hex is not ancient like some mathematical games. It was invented in the 1940s, less than 100 years ago. Two different mathematicians, Piet Hein and John Nash, came up with the same idea separately. Hex is tricky because as well as trying to make your own chain, you're trying to block your opponent—and they're trying to block you, too!

GREAT mathematical minds think alike!

TWO COIN GAMES

For these games, all you need is a big pile of coins or counters and two players. For the first game, Subtract a Square, you also need to know about square numbers.

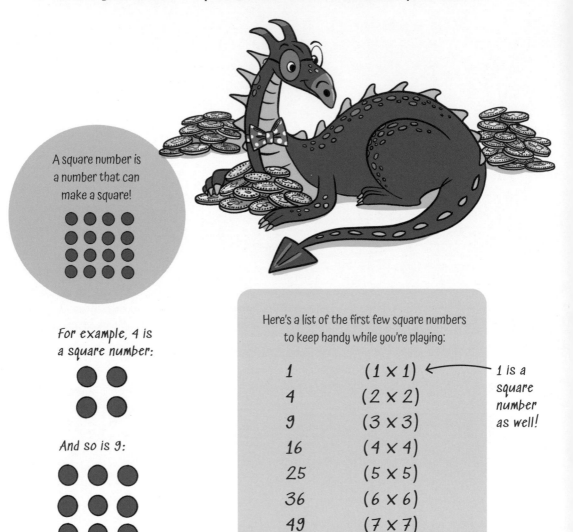

A square number is a number that can make a square!

For example, 4 is a square number:

And so is 9:

All square numbers are the result of multiplying a number by itself. So, for example, 9 is 3 × 3.

Here's a list of the first few square numbers to keep handy while you're playing:

1	(1 × 1)
4	(2 × 2)
9	(3 × 3)
16	(4 × 4)
25	(5 × 5)
36	(6 × 6)
49	(7 × 7)
64	(8 × 8)
81	(9 × 9)
100	(10 × 10)

1 is a square number as well!

SUBTRACT A SQUARE

 1 Put any number of coins in a pile, then take turns playing.

4 coins

2 When it's your turn, you have to take away a square number of coins. So you could take away 1, 4, 9, or 16 coins—or even 100, if there are enough in the pile.

The player who takes the last coin is the winner.

Game science

Once you get down to fewer than 20 coins, it's a smart game of strategy to make your opponent end up with two coins. They have no choice but to take one, and you win!

MONEY PILES

This is a similar game, but you have two piles of coins instead of one.

1 Split your coins into two separate piles. The piles don't have to be the same size.

Sounds simple, but you'll soon find it's super tricky!

2 To play, each player takes turns removing some coins, as in Subtract a Square. But the rules are different:

- You can take any number of coins from one pile or both piles.

- If you take coins from both piles, you have to take the same number from each pile.

- The winner is the one who takes the last coin.

FLIP IT!

This game comes in many forms and has many different names. Some say it's thousands of years old, but new versions have been invented more recently, and one version exists as the board game Othello.

Set it up

1 You play the game on a grid with eight squares on each side, making 64 squares in total. It's easy to draw one on paper or cardboard using a pencil and a ruler—or you might be able to print out one you've found online.

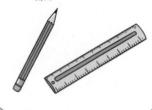

What do you need?

- Paper or cardboard
- Ruler
- Pencil
- Scissors
- Glue

2 You also need 64 counters. Each counter must have a black side and a white side (or a blue side and a red side—or any other combination).

Make your counters by cutting circles out of two shades of card and sticking them together.

3 The players choose black or white, and they take turns putting a counter on the board their way up.

How to play

 4 The first four moves must be played in the four middle squares, like this, to get you started.

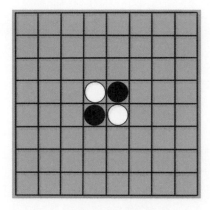

 5 After that, whenever you play a move, you have to trap one or more of your opponent's counters between your counters in a straight line (vertical, horizontal, or diagonal). Here's an example:

Ha ha, got ya!

 6 Then you flip the "trapped" piece or pieces to switch them to your own shade.

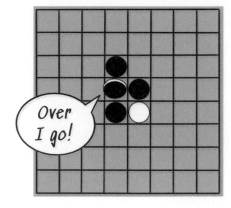

Over I go!

 7 If you can't play a move, you miss a turn. If neither player can play, the game is over.

The winner is the one who has the most counters facing their way up when the game ends.

Game science

Every time a counter gets trapped, it gets flipped—so each counter can flip over many times during a game. Try to trap the longest possible row of your opponent's pieces.

KAYLES

What is a kayle? It's similar to a bowling pin, and this game is based on knocking down a row of them. You don't even need a bowling ball!

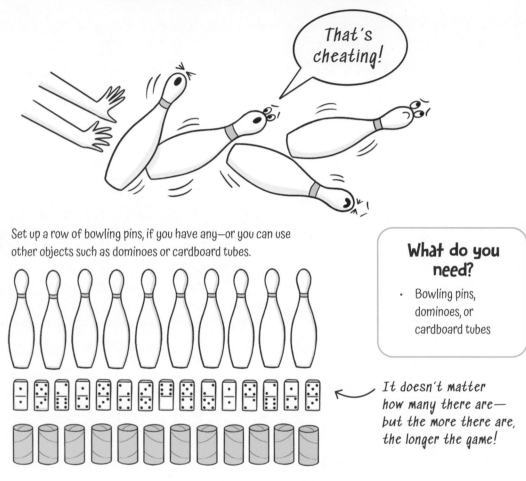

That's cheating!

1 Set up a row of bowling pins, if you have any—or you can use other objects such as dominoes or cardboard tubes.

What do you need?

- Bowling pins, dominoes, or cardboard tubes

It doesn't matter how many there are—but the more there are, the longer the game!

2 The two players take turns knocking the kayles down. When it's your turn, you can knock down one kayle or two that are side by side.

3 The winner is the one who knocks over the last kayle!

Game science

Kayles was invented in 1908 by puzzle-crazy mathematics expert Henry Dudeney. It's another game with simple rules that requires clever strategy to win! You need to try and end up with one kayle on its own or two kayles side by side. Make your moves carefully!

15 PEBBLES

Here's a puzzling pebble game to play on paper.

 1 Draw 15 pebbles on a piece of paper.

What do you need?

- Paper
- Pencil
- Two different pens or crayons

2 Each player decides how they will decorate their pebbles. In the example, one player is green and the other silver.

3 When it's your turn, you can fill in one, two, or three pebbles. It's up to you! The aim is to end up with an odd number of pebbles—NOT an even number.

4 When all the pebbles are done, count up how many each person has. If you have an odd number, you're the winner!

Silver wins!

CODE CRACKER

In this two-player game, you become a spy, cracking the code to figure out your opponent's secret number.

What do you need?

- Pad
- Paper
- Ruler

1 Player one must think of a four-digit number. Write it down without player two seeing it. Let's say it's 2873.

Fold it up and keep it safe.

2 On the pad of paper, draw a grid like this, with four columns for the four numbers:

3 Now player two has to guess what the number is. They'll have to start with a random guess, like 4857. They should write their guess at the top of the grid.

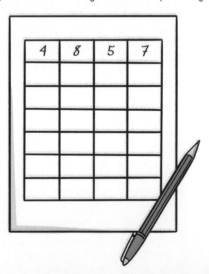

4 Now, player one checks the guess—and adds symbols to each number.

A CHECK ✓

... means the right number in the right place.

A STAR *

... means the right number in the WRONG place.

And a CROSS through the number X

... means the number is completely wrong.

5 Armed with this knowledge, player two can now take another guess.

They'll keep the 8, since that's right.

They'll keep the 7 but try putting it somewhere else.

They'll drop the 4 and 5, since they're wrong, and try other numbers.

They're getting closer! 6 is wrong, but 8 and 7 are now both in the right place, and there is a 2, though it's not in the right place.

6 Player one marks up the new number with the special symbols, and player two tries again until they crack it!

It's 2873! You got me!

Then swap places and play again. The winner is the one who cracks the code in the fewest guesses.

Game science

In this game, you win by keeping track of all the previous numbers and whether they were right or wrong. Don't just keep guessing—use all the clues!

Prime
power!

PRIME SNAP

You've probably played Snap, but have you played MATHEMATICAL Snap?

Set it up

1 For these games, you need a set of cards numbered from 1–50. To make them, cut rectangles from cardboard, and write the numbers on them with a marker. Or you could use an old pack of normal playing cards that you don't need, then write the numbers on them.

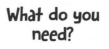

What do you need?

- Cardboard or old set of playing cards
- Scissors
- Marker

2 Prime Snap works using prime numbers. They are numbers that can only be divided by themselves and one.

1	2	3	4	5	6	7	8	9	10
11	12	13	14	15	16	17	18	19	20
21	22	23	24	25	26	27	28	29	30
31	32	33	34	35	36	37	38	39	40
41	42	43	44	45	46	47	48	49	50
51	52	53	54	55	56	57	58	59	60
61	62	63	64	65	66	67	68	69	70
71	72	73	74	75	76	77	78	79	80
81	82	83	84	85	86	87	88	89	90
91	92	93	94	95	96	97	98	99	100

There are 25 prime numbers between 1 and 100. You can see them all here.

How to play

3 Deal the cards into two piles, face down. The players take one pile each, then take turns turning over a card and putting it in the middle.

4 When it's a prime number, the first to yell "PRIME!" gets to take the middle pile.

5 The game ends when one person runs out of cards—the other is the winner!

TIMES TABLE SNAP

Use the same set of cards to play Times Table Snap.

1 In this game, instead of prime numbers, you're looking for numbers that belong to a times table. Before you start, pick a table—for example, the five times table.

2 When you see a number from the five times table come up, the first to shout out the number—such as "25!"—gets to take the pile.

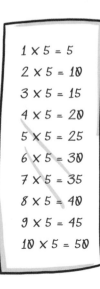

$$1 \times 5 = 5$$
$$2 \times 5 = 10$$
$$3 \times 5 = 15$$
$$4 \times 5 = 20$$
$$5 \times 5 = 25$$
$$6 \times 5 = 30$$
$$7 \times 5 = 35$$
$$8 \times 5 = 40$$
$$9 \times 5 = 45$$
$$10 \times 5 = 50$$

Try this, too!

Too easy? Make it harder by making a set of cards up to 100!

DICE DUEL

I challenge you to a duel—a dice duel! For this game, you have to think fast.

Dice at dawn!

I accept your challenge!

What do you need?

- Cardboard or old cereal box
- Ruler
- Marker or pencil
- Scissors
- Two dice
- Flat tray
- Box

Set it up

First, make two sets of cards by cutting small rectangles from a piece of cardboard or an old cereal box. Draw numbers on them with a thick marker.

2 3 4 5 6 7 8 9 10 11 12 ← *Each player needs 11 cards numbered from 2–12, like this.*

How to play

2 To play, each player lines their cards up in front of them and takes one dice.

3 On the count of three, you both roll your dice into the tray. (This keeps the dice together and keeps them from rolling off somewhere.)

4 Quickly add up the numbers on the two dice to get the total. For example, if you've rolled a two and a five, the total is seven.

5 Try to be the first to grab the seven from your row of cards, and put it in the tray.

6 If the other player gets theirs in first, you have to take your card back and keep it.

7 But if a player tries to put the wrong card in, they have to take the card back, too. So if you use your seven, but they use their six, you win the point and get to put your card in, even if you were slower.

Remember ...

As you're playing, your cards will start to get used up. If you've played your seven, and the dice show seven again, you can't play. If the other player still has their seven, they can!

8 Keep playing the same way until one person has no cards left. They're the winner!

Game science

The fewer cards you have left, the less chance the dice will roll a number you can play—which could lead to a nail-biting finish!

NINE MEN'S MORRIS

Take a trip to ancient Rome with a game of Nine Men's Morris!
The Romans loved to play this, and it's been popular ever since.

Set it up

 Copy this playing board onto a piece of paper or cardboard.

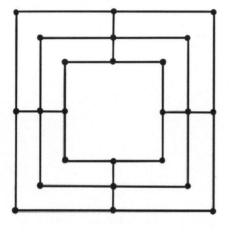

I came,
I saw...
I won!

 You also need some playing pieces—nine black and nine white (these are the "nine men"). You could make them from cardboard, or use counters from a game you already have.

What do you need?

- Paper or cardboard
- Marker or pencil
- Scissors
- Nine white counters
- Nine black counters

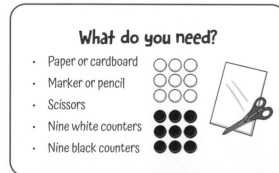

How to play

 Decide who's going to play black and who's playing white.

 To start the game, the players take turns putting one of their pieces down on the dots.

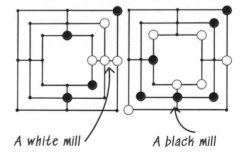

A white mill   A black mill

Your aim is to make rows of three, connected by a straight line—like the ones you can see here. A row of three is called a "mill."

5 Whenever you make a mill, you can take one of your opponent's pieces off the board. You can't take a piece from one of their mills, unless there are no others to take.

6 When both players have put down all their pieces, they take turns moving one of their pieces. They can only move along the lines from one dot to an empty dot next to it. (No jumping over pieces or hopping between lines.)

For example, you could move this piece from here ...

... to here.

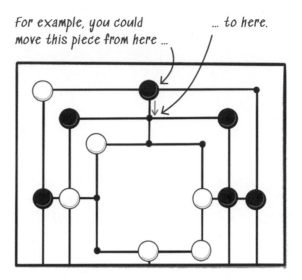

7 With each move, keep trying to make more mills (straight lines of three). Every time you create a new mill, you get to take another of your opponent's pieces.

8 The game ends when one player has only two pieces left and can't make mills—or when neither player can move. The one with the most pieces left is the winner.

What's a morris?

This game might get its English name from the Morris dance, a traditional folk dance. Or it could have come from the Latin word "merellus," which means a playing piece.

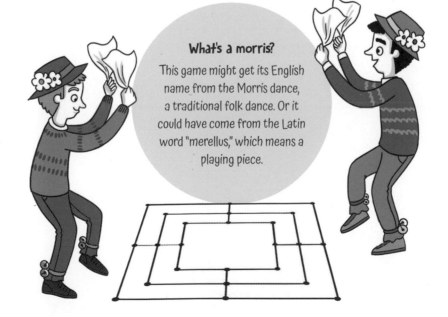

REBEL ARMY

This traditional two-player game comes from China.
One person plays as the general, and the other is the rebel army.

Set it up

 1 Here's the board for the game of Rebel Army. It's a grid of 16 squares, with diagonal lines across them. You will need to make a copy of this board.

2 You also need 16 white counters for the rebel army and one black one for the general. Use counters from another game, or just make your own from cardboard.

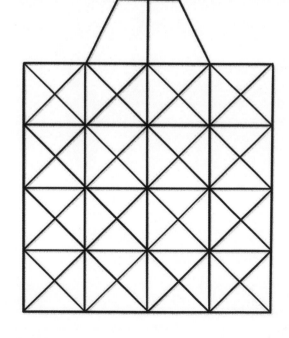

What do you need?

- Paper or cardboard
- Marker or pencil
- 16 white counters and one black counter (or whichever two shades you prefer)

Set up the counters on the board like this. The triangle at the top is the general's private hideaway. Only the general can enter.

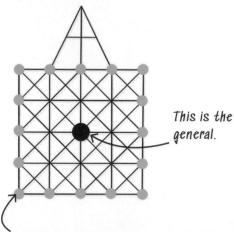

This is the general.

The rebel army is made up of 16 pieces.

How to play

3 Players take turns moving a piece along a line, to an empty spot.

You can only move one space at a time. The general can only move one piece, but the other player can move any of the rebels.

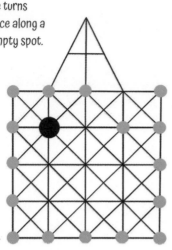

4 If you're the rebels, your aim is to surround the general and block him in, so that he can't move.

You can surround him with pieces, or trap him against the edge of the board. →

5 The general captures rebels by moving in between two rebels to form a straight line, like this:

General moves between two rebels.

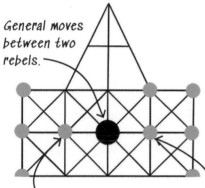

He captures both rebels and removes them from the board!

6 If you're the general, you can win in two ways.

EITHER:
- Escape to the point of the triangle in your hideaway. However, the rebels win if they can block you in by taking up the three spots at the base of the triangle.

OR:
- Capture so many rebels that they can't block you in.

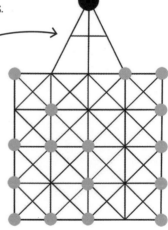

Game science

You might think it's pretty unfair that the general only has one piece, but because he can capture, it's possible for him to win. Try playing and see what happens!

CHANCE DICE

Dice are essential for all kinds of games, and you can play some brilliant mathematical games with them too. Here's a super-simple (yet very tricky!) one-dice game to start you off.

How to play

1 Your aim is to throw the dice again and again, writing down each score and adding them up to try and get it as high as possible.

So, for example, you might throw this sequence:

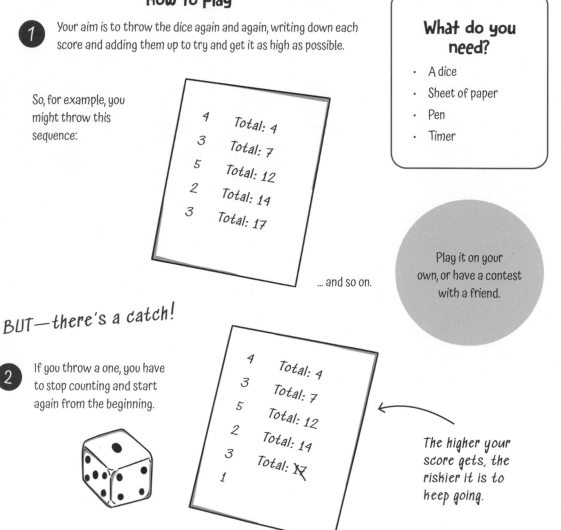

4	Total: 4
3	Total: 7
5	Total: 12
2	Total: 14
3	Total: 17

... and so on.

What do you need?

- A dice
- Sheet of paper
- Pen
- Timer

Play it on your own, or have a contest with a friend.

BUT—there's a catch!

2 If you throw a one, you have to stop counting and start again from the beginning.

4	Total: 4
3	Total: 7
5	Total: 12
2	Total: 14
3	Total: 17
1	

The higher your score gets, the riskier it is to keep going.

AGAINST THE CLOCK

3 To play against the clock, set the timer for three minutes, and get going!

4 When the time is up, the score you have at that moment is your total. Do you stick with a good score, such as 28, or take a chance and try to get it a little higher?

5 To play against someone else, all the players start at the same time when you set the timer. You can even play in teams of two, with one roller and one scorekeeper. Each player or team will need a dice, pen, and some paper.

It's high up here!

6 The winner is the person or team with the highest score when the timer sounds!

Game science

This game is all about probability—how likely you are to roll a one. With every roll, there's a one in six chance. This means it's hard to build up a score higher than about 25, unless you're very lucky. Try it and see!

SEQUENCE SPOTTER

The rules to this game are simple—spot the pattern in the sequence of numbers.
Try solving these first, then create your own to challenge your friends.

Start counting out loud from one
... NOW!

Are you counting yet?
What did you say?

Was it:
1, 2, 3, 4, 5, 6, 7, 8, 9, 10 ... and so on? Hope so!

This is a number sequence—a set of numbers in order. In this case, it's the basic whole number sequence, which we use for everyday things like house numbers. We all know it because we start learning it as babies. But there are other number sequences, too ...

How to play

 Try solving these sequence puzzles. They start off quite easy, then get harder! For each one, you have to figure out how the sequence works, then fill in the missing numbers.

Here's an example:

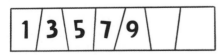

Did you spot it? You just add two each time.
So the next numbers are 11 and 13.

Here's another:

In this sequence, you add three each time.
The answers are 23 and 26.

A LITTLE BIT HARDER ...

Now you're on your own! (But you can check the answers at the end of the book.)

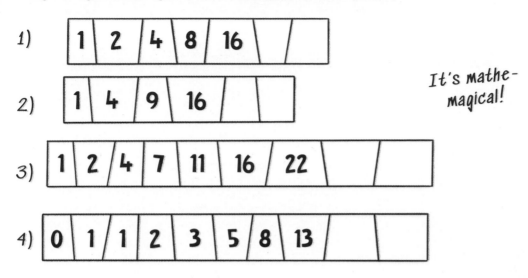

1) | 1 | 2 | 4 | 8 | 16 | | |

2) | 1 | 4 | 9 | 16 | | | |

3) | 1 | 2 | 4 | 7 | 11 | 16 | 22 | | |

4) | 0 | 1 | 1 | 2 | 3 | 5 | 8 | 13 | | |

It's mathe-magical!

Create your own!

Now that you know how it works, you can think up your own sneaky number sequences for someone else to crack. Here are a few ideas ...

- A number sequence that gets lower instead of higher
- A sequence that uses multiplying instead of adding
- A sequence that uses fractions or decimal numbers

Game science

There are thousands of sequences like this, and mathematicians love messing around with them and thinking up new ones. For every sequence, there's a rule, such as "add 2" or "add one more number than you did last time," and once you figure out what the rule is, you can use it to predict what comes next.

BACTERIA BOOM

Bacteria are tiny living things with only one cell each. Some are germs and cause illnesses, while others are harmless or even helpful. But what matters here is how they multiply!

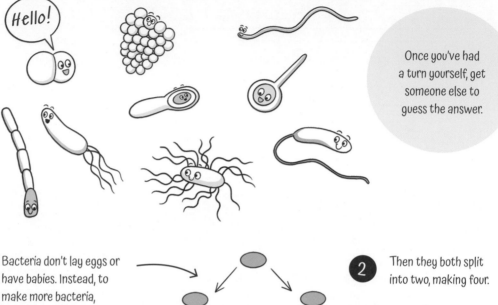

Hello!

Once you've had a turn yourself, get someone else to guess the answer.

1 Bacteria don't lay eggs or have babies. Instead, to make more bacteria, one bacterium splits into two.

2 Then they both split into two, making four.

3 Imagine that the bacteria did this once a day.

Does this look familiar? You might recognize it as one of the sequences from the previous page. Well spotted!

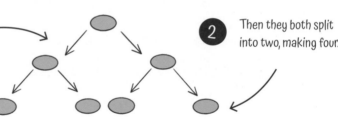

On day 1, there would be ...	
On day 2, there would be ...	
On day 3, there would be ...	
On day 4, there would be ...	
On day 5, there would be ...	

Leave them to it, and eventually there will be over a million bacteria!

 4 So the question is ... when do you think that would happen? If there's one bacterium on day one, which day will it be when they pass the one million (1,000,000) mark?

Day 100 maybe?
Day 365 (a whole year)?
Or sooner?

Guess which day, then use a calculator to check.

When do you get past a million? The answer might surprise you!

Day 1   1
Day 2   1 x 2 = 2
Day 3   2 x 2 = 4
Day 4   4 x 2 = 8
Day 5   8 x 2 = 16
Day 6   16 x 2 = 32
Day 7   32 x 2 = 64
Day 8   64 x 2 = 128
Day 9...

Game science

As you can see, when you double the number each time, it grows slowly at first—but soon it's shooting up! In fact, you should go past 1 million on day 21. And just ten days later, on day 31, the number will pass 1 BILLION (1,000,000,000).

In mathematics, this kind of growth, made by doubling a number again and again, is called exponential growth.

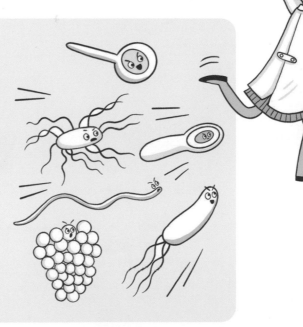

TRAFFIC POINTS

This is a game for playing when you're on a car trip and feeling a bit bored. You can also play it while you're walking along a road or even just looking out of a window.

How to play

1. Each type of red vehicle on the road has a number of points. You can make up your own points system, or use this one:

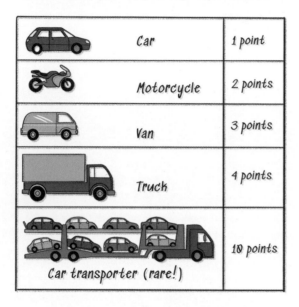

	Car	1 point
	Motorcycle	2 points
	Van	3 points
	Truck	4 points
	Car transporter (rare!)	10 points

One or more people can play (but not the driver—they should concentrate on what they're doing!).

What do you need?

- Just your eyes and brain!

2. Every time you spot a red vehicle, add the points to your total, keeping the score in your head. See if you can beat a target score by the time you get to your destination, or just see how high you can get.

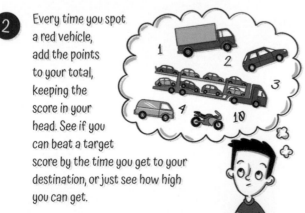

3. If there's more than one person, you can work together, or play against each other. To do this, each person decides if they will spot red, blue, or white vehicles.

4 Each person then looks out for only their own vehicles and adds the points to their own score.

The person with the highest score wins!

This game is easy, but great as a way to improve your mental arithmetic (in other words, your ability to do equations inside your head!).

You might also find that some types of vehicles are MUCH more common than others. Why do you think that is?

Try this, too!

You could invent similar games for types of plants or trees on a country walk, or types of pebbles or seashells you can find at the beach.

MEASURE HUNT

This isn't a treasure hunt—it's a measure hunt!

Play on your own, against each other, or in teams—and play indoors for the best results.

What do you need?

- Large piece of cardboard or string
- Ruler or tape measure
- Pencil
- Scissors

How to play

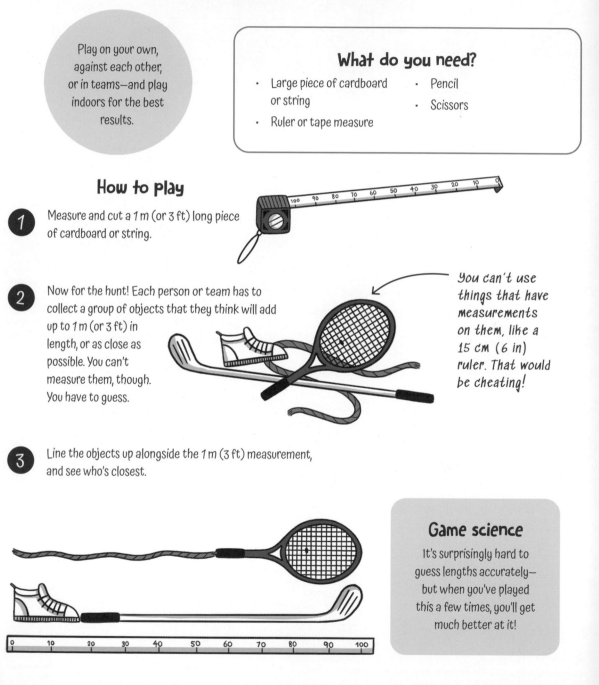

1 Measure and cut a 1 m (or 3 ft) long piece of cardboard or string.

2 Now for the hunt! Each person or team has to collect a group of objects that they think will add up to 1 m (or 3 ft) in length, or as close as possible. You can't measure them, though. You have to guess.

You can't use things that have measurements on them, like a 15 cm (6 in) ruler. That would be cheating!

3 Line the objects up alongside the 1 m (3 ft) measurement, and see who's closest.

Game science

It's surprisingly hard to guess lengths accurately—but when you've played this a few times, you'll get much better at it!

SMOOTS

In 1958, some students decided to measure the Harvard Bridge in Massachusetts, USA. But instead of using feet or meters, they used their friend, Oliver Smoot!

Smoot lay down while the others marked his length, then they repeated this all the way across the bridge. It was 364.4 Smoots long!

To this day, Oliver Smoot's height at the time, 170 cm (5 ft 7 in), is known as one Smoot.

How to play

 To play Smoots, pick an object (or a person, if they don't mind!), and guess how many of them there are in a particular distance—such as the length of a room.

1 Aunt Ruth

2 Write down your guess, then use your object to measure the distance and see how close you were!

BINARY RACE

Binary, or base 2, is a counting system. All numbers,
no matter how big, can be boiled down to a series of 0s and 1s.

We normally use the base 10 system,
which has 10 number symbols:

But binary has just two symbols:

Base 10

Base 2

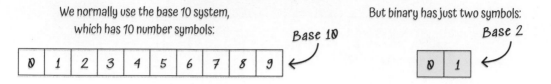

0	1	2	3	4	5	6	7	8	9

0	1

In base 10, you use the symbols 0–9,
then start again from 10, using two columns.

In binary, you use just 0 and 1, and then start again,
using two columns to show the number 2.

For example,
the number 11
means:

11	
10's	1's
• • • • •	•
One 10	One 1
1	1

11	
2's	1's
• •	•
One 2	One 1
1	1

In base 10, each column is 10 times bigger
than the next column.

But in binary, each column is only two
times bigger than the next column.

1,000's	100's	10's	1's

8's	4's	2's	1's

To change a number to binary,
you divide it into these columns.
For example ...

5

	8's	4's	2's	1's	
		• • • •		•	
		One 4	No 2's	One 1	
		1	0	1	... or 101

5 in binary is:

14

	8's	4's	2's	1's	
	• • • • • • • •	• • • •	• •		
	One 8	One 4	One 2	no 1's	
	1	1	1	0	... or 1110

14 in binary is:

How to play

1 Write the binary columns along the top of the paper, like this:

16's	8's	4's	2's	1's

Each player needs:

- 30 small coins or counters
- Pen or pencil
- Piece of paper

2 Next, choose any number up to 30. Each player takes that many counters.

You can play on your own, or race against other people.

3 Then, on the count of three, start sorting them into the columns.

If you have enough, put 16 in the 16's column.
If there are enough left, put 8 in the 8's column.
If not, move to the 4's column ... and so on.

4 When you've used all the coins, write 1's and 0's for each column.
For example, if your number was 21, it would look like this:

16's	8's	4's	2's	1's
● ● ● ● ● ● ● ● ● ● ● ● ● ●		● ● ● ●		●
1	0	1	0	1

So 21 in base 10 = 10101 in binary!
The first to get each answer scores a point.

BINARY FLIP

Once you're used to binary, try playing high-speed Binary Flip!

How to play

1 For each player, cut five rectangles from a piece of cardboard (or cardboard box).

2 Now draw dots on the cards, like this.

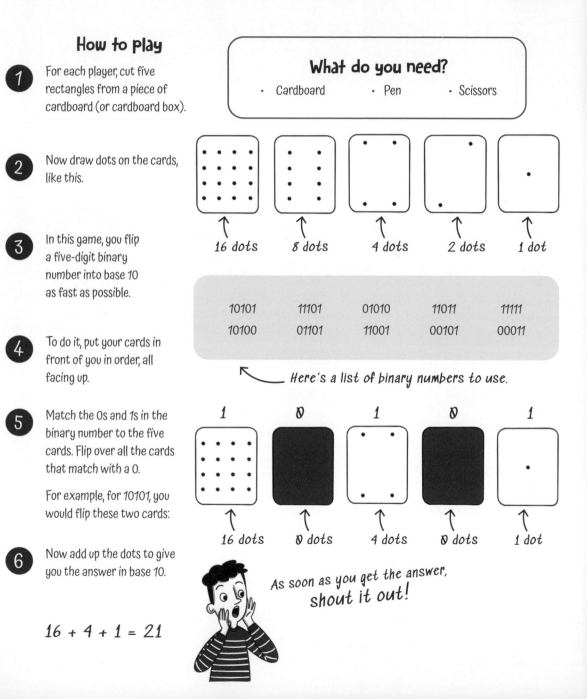

16 dots   8 dots   4 dots   2 dots   1 dot

3 In this game, you flip a five-digit binary number into base 10 as fast as possible.

| 10101 | 11101 | 01010 | 11011 | 11111 |
| 10100 | 01101 | 11001 | 00101 | 00011 |

4 To do it, put your cards in front of you in order, all facing up.

Here's a list of binary numbers to use.

5 Match the 0s and 1s in the binary number to the five cards. Flip over all the cards that match with a 0.

For example, for 10101, you would flip these two cards:

1   0   1   0   1

16 dots   0 dots   4 dots   0 dots   1 dot

6 Now add up the dots to give you the answer in base 10.

As soon as you get the answer, **shout it out!**

16 + 4 + 1 = 21

38

BINARY SECRET CODE

Computers use binary to do calculations. They work by switching a flow of electricity on and off. On stands for 1, and off stands for 0!

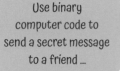

Use binary computer code to send a secret message to a friend ...

 1 Computers use eight-digit binary numbers, or "ASCII" numbers, to stand for the letters of the alphabet—and here they are!

A:	01000001	J:	01001010	S:	01010010
B:	01000010	K:	01001011	T:	01010010
C:	01000011	L:	01001100	U:	01010101
D:	01000100	M:	01001101	V:	01010110
E:	01000101	N:	01001110	W:	01010111
F:	01000110	O:	01001111	X:	01011000
G:	01000111	P:	01010000	Y:	01011001
H:	01001000	Q:	01010001	Z:	01011010
I:	01001001	R:	01010010		

2 To write a coded message, write down the binary code for each letter.

3 Write them all down in a long string with no gaps.

01010010010000101010100111001000100001000110010011110100011110100001 00

Any spy who intercepts your code will just see a jumble of 0's and 1's!

4 To decode the message, your friend separates the numbers into blocks of eight ...

01010010 / 01000101 /
01001110 / 01000100 /
01000110 / 01001111 /
01001111 / 01000100

... then finds the right alphabet letters from the list!

01010010 = S / 01000101 = E /
01001110 = N / 01000100 = D /
01000110 = F / 01001111 = O /
01001111 = O / 01000100 = D

39

PI CHALLENGE

Pi is an important number in mathematics ... but it's also kind of strange.

Pi isn't a "whole" number like 2, 4, or 5. Instead, it's somewhere between 3 and 4. Even stranger, it's never-ending ...

What is pi?

Pi comes from a simple calculation:

The circumference of a circle (the distance around the edge)

... divided by its diameter (the distance across the middle).

Written down, pi starts like this:

3.141592653589793238 46264338327950288419711693993753105...

Mathematicians also show pi using this symbol:

π

 Your challenge is to memorize as many digits of pi as possible by creating your own sentence. Each word in your sentence should have the same number of letters in it as the number you want to remember.

 Here are the first 10 digits—could you make them into a sentence?

3.141592653

The weirder the sentence, the easier it will be to remember. Here's one!

Dad,	I	drew	a	green	chameleon	on	Mabel's	magic	hat!
3.	1	4	1	5	9	2	6	5	3

3 Can you do a better one, or a longer one?

See how many digits of Pi you can learn, or have a contest.

PI STRINGS

For this game, you just need string, scissors, round objects, and pi!

Take turns with a friend or family member, and see who gets closest.

1 Find some round objects, such as bowls, pans, or food cans.

2 Cut a piece of string that will fit perfectly around the object—without measuring it!

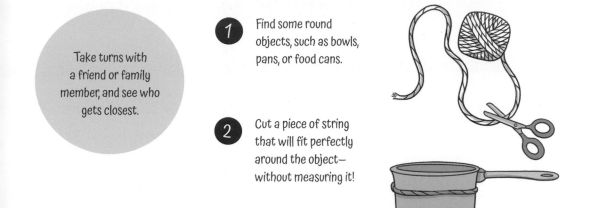

4 9 4 4 5 9 2 3 0 7 8 1 6 4 0 6 2 8 6 2 0 8 9 9 8 6 2 8 0 3 4 8 2 5 3 4 2 1 1 7 0 6 7 9 8 2 1 4 8 0 8 6 5

3 Guess the circumference by looking at the width or diameter of the object, then cut a piece of string about 3.14 times longer. How close can you get?

Almost!

41

LOOPS

Loops is a mathematics game to play on paper.
It has simple rules, but it'll drive you loopy!

How to play

1 The game starts off as a grid with the numbers 0, 1, 2, or 3 dotted around on it.

Here's a very small, easy one to show how it works. →

3	2
2	3

What do you need?

- Graph paper
- Pen or pencil

2 To solve the puzzle, draw along the lines of the grid to make a connected loop. The numbers show you how many sides of each box you have to draw along.

Here's a solution to the puzzle above:

3	2
2	3

Here's your loop.
"3" boxes have lines drawn on three sides.
"2" boxes have lines drawn on two sides.

3 Once you've got the idea, try these ...

```
        3
   3  0     1
   3  2
      2  2
```

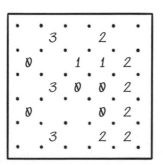

```
   3      2
 0    1  1  2
    3  0  0  2
 0        0  2
    3     2  2
```

```
            2
 2  3     0  3
    3  1  1
 1        3  1
 2  0     2
            1  1
```

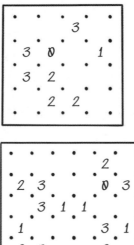

Try making your own Loops puzzles on graph paper, to challenge your friends or family.

BAG

Is mathematics your bag? Like Loops, the game of Bag is played on a grid of any size.

 1 This time, you draw your loop, or "bag," around all the numbers. The numbers show how many squares each number must have around it, including the one it's on and all the squares up, down, left, and right from it.

Here's an easy example:

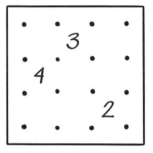

And here's the answer!

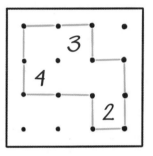

The 3 has three boxes: the one it's on, one below it, and one to the left.
The 4 has the one it's on, one above it, and two to the right.
The 2 has the one it's on and the one above it.

Solved!

2 Here are some more to try ...

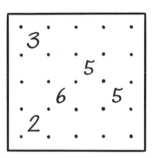

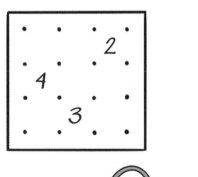

KAKURO

If you like mathematics and you like crosswords, you'll LOVE Kakuro! It's a Japanese puzzle game that's played on a crossword-like grid, with numbers instead of letters.

How to play

1 Like many other grid games, a Kakuro game can be any size. They're often played on grids that are 8 x 8 squares or larger, but you can have smaller ones, too. Here's a mini-Kakuro to start you off.

You don't fill in the black squares.

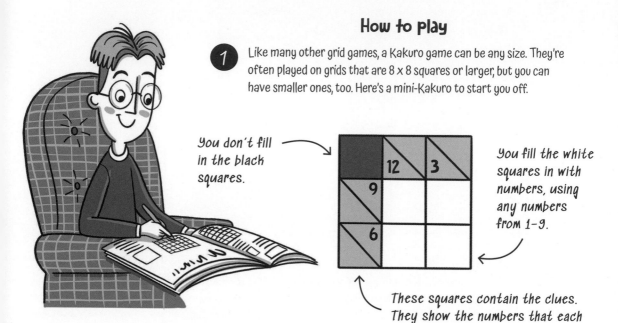

You fill the white squares in with numbers, using any numbers from 1-9.

These squares contain the clues. They show the numbers that each row and column have to add up to.

For example, this 12 means that the numbers in the column below it must add up to 12.

And this 9 means that the numbers in the row next to it must add up to 9 ... and so on.

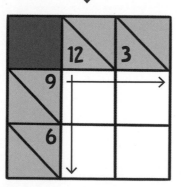

This is one solution. There's another one that works, too—can you figure it out?

Once you know what you're doing, get going with these clever Kakuro challenges!

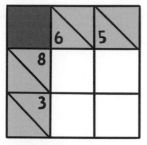

A

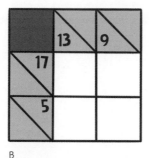

B

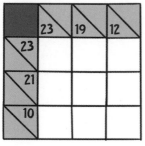

C

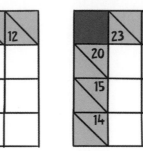

D

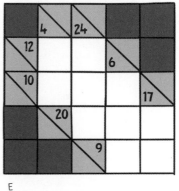

E

Game science

Kakuro is a little like a magic square in which all the rows, columns, and diagonal rows of numbers add up to the same number. This is an ancient idea in mathematics that features in old legends. In one Chinese legend, a turtle came out of a river with a magic square on its back!

You can count on me!

TESSELLATION TILES

If a shape tessellates, that means you can use it like a tile to fill a space with no gaps, like this!

How to play

1 Check out our shape selection. Can you tell which ones will tessellate and which won't?

You can try this on your own, or challenge a friend to a race!

Triangle

Octagon

Five-pointed star

Wide H

Arrow

Blobby balloon

2 Write down your answers on some paper. If you're playing against a friend, use one piece of paper each.

No peeking!

Test it!

3 Trace or carefully copy each shape onto cardboard, and cut it out (a cereal box will do). To see if a shape tessellates, draw around it onto paper, then draw more of them and see if you can make them fit together. (If it goes wrong, just start again.)

IT TAKES TWO!

Sometimes, two different shapes can work together to make a tessellating pattern.

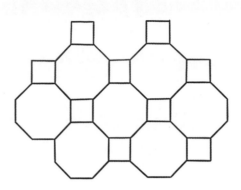

How to play

 Your challenge is to find out which two of these shapes will tessellate together.

Pentagon

Oval

Four-sided diamond

Rectangle

Five-sided diamond

Guess first, then copy the shapes and see if you can crack it!

Try this too!

Can you create your own brand-new tessellating shape?

Game science

Tessellation is all about angles. However weird they look, and however you arrange them, your shapes must have angles that fit together at the corners.

Ouch!

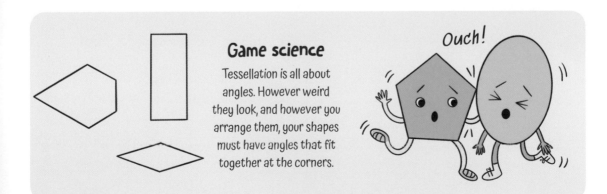

TANGRAM TEASERS

Tangram is an old Chinese game made from a square divided up into simple shapes.

Play on your own, or race against other people (each person needs their own set).

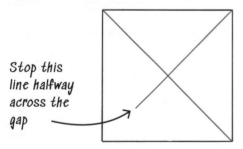

What do you need?

- Cardboard or craft foam
- Ruler
- Marker or pencil
- Scissors

Set it up

1 Use the ruler to mark out a square 10 x 10 cm (4 x 4 in) on your cardboard or foam.

2 Draw diagonal lines across the square in an X shape, like this.

Stop this line halfway across the gap

3 Measure and mark the halfway points on some of the lines, as shown in this diagram.

4 Connect the marks to make a pattern of shapes, like this.

5 Cut your Tangram into separate shapes.

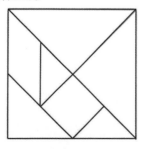

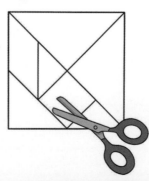

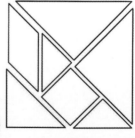

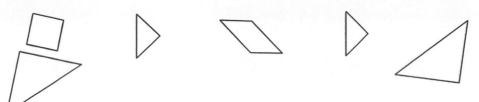

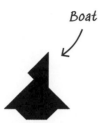

How to play

6 To solve a Tangram puzzle, try and make a shape when you can only see its outline, by figuring out which pieces go where. Here are some to try!

Boat

Rocket

House

Rabbit

Chicken →

   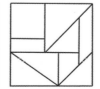

Runner

Wow!

CREATE YOUR OWN TANGRAM

Now make your own! Start with another 10 x 10 cm (4 x 4 in) square, but this time, design your own puzzle pieces by dividing it up in a different way. What pictures can you make with your new set?

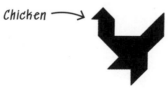

Game science

The original Tangram is carefully designed so that whatever picture you want to make, there are pieces that will work for the different parts. But could it be even better?

BLOCK BUILDER

For this game, you need squared or graph paper. You can buy it at a stationery store, or find some on the internet and print it out.

Set it up

1 Draw a rectangle to make a playing board. Ten squares long and six squares high is a good size to start with.

2 Take some more graph paper and cut it up into playing pieces, each made of three squares. There are two shapes you can make, known as "triominoes." For a 10 x 6 square board, make 10 of each shape, using 60 squares in total.

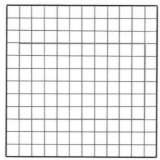

Play this on your own or with an opponent.

How to play

3 Start putting the pieces onto the board, fitting them together to cover the squares. Can you fit them all on? If not, how close can you get?

Game science

The pieces CAN all fit on the board, but only if you figure out the right way to arrange them. If you're playing an opponent, try to make it harder for them by blocking their best moves!

4 To play with someone else, toss a coin to see who goes first, then take turns adding one shape at a time. If you can't play, you lose!

HMMM...

TETRA BLOCKS

Too easy? Let's try the game again, but this time using four-square "tetrominoes" and a bigger playing board.

1 Try doing the same thing, but make four-square pieces instead.

There are seven possible four-square tetrominoes.

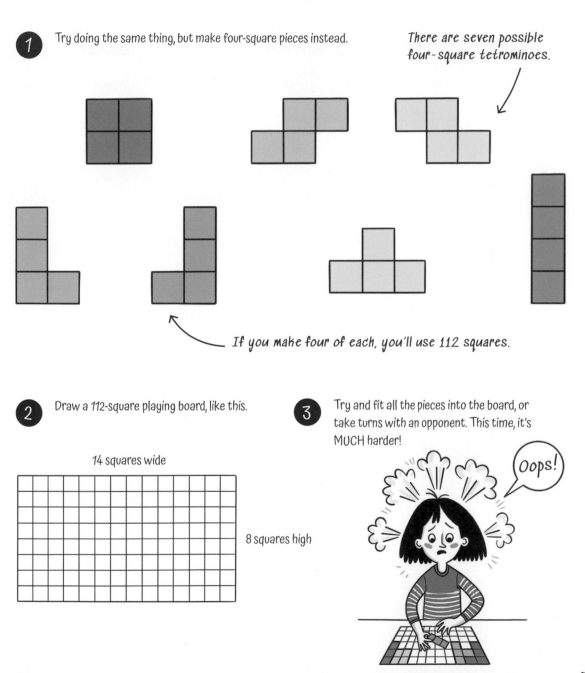

If you make four of each, you'll use 112 squares.

2 Draw a 112-square playing board, like this.

14 squares wide

8 squares high

3 Try and fit all the pieces into the board, or take turns with an opponent. This time, it's MUCH harder!

Oops!

MIRROR MATCHER

A symmetrical shape is the same on both sides. One side is like a mirror image of the other. This game is a race to match both halves of a symmetrical shape together.

This works best if you set a challenge for someone else or race against them.

What do you need?

- Thin cardboard, such as a cereal box
- Pencil
- Scissors

Set it up

1 Cut the cardboard into 8–10 cm (3–4 in) squares.

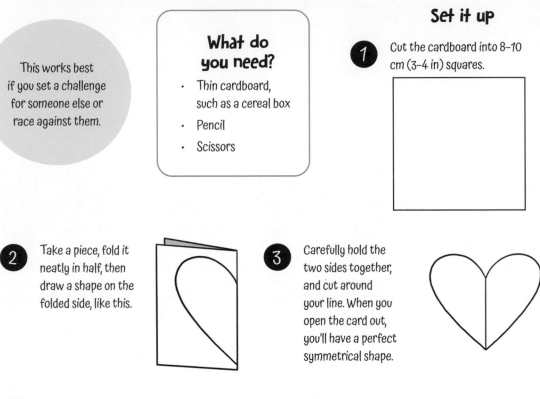

2 Take a piece, fold it neatly in half, then draw a shape on the folded side, like this.

3 Carefully hold the two sides together, and cut around your line. When you open the card out, you'll have a perfect symmetrical shape.

4 Make lots more symmetrical shapes in the same way. They can be whatever you like!

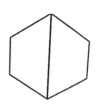
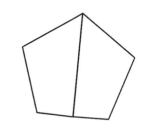

5 When that's done, cut all your shapes in half, right along the fold. Put one half of each shape on a tray or plate and the other half in a bag or box, so you can't see it.

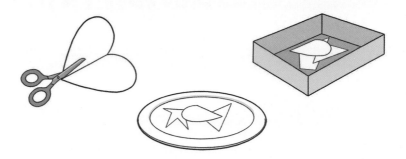

How to play

6 To play, close your eyes and take a piece out of the bag or box. Then try to find the matching piece as quickly as possible!

Tricky!

7 If you have two or more players, each person takes a piece. Then, on the count of three, you all have to race to find your matching piece in the pile. First to find it scores a point!

Game science

The more complicated the shapes are, the harder it will be to spot the right matching half To make it extra tricky, design some symmetrical shapes that are similar, but not quite the same as each other.

GRAPH CODE

A graph is a squared grid with numbers along the bottom (the x axis) and side (the y axis). The numbers line up with lines on the graph. You can mark a point on the graph using two numbers, one from each axis.

How to play

1 Draw a simple picture like this, with all the corners at points where lines cross. It should be a picture that you can draw as one continuous line.

2 Now mark all the corners and write them down in a list. For example, the first three in this picture are:

X5, Y7
X6, Y8
X7, Y8

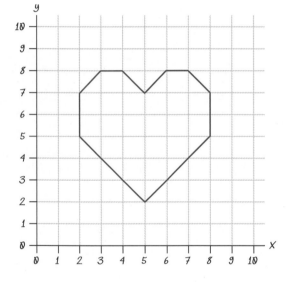

3 To crack the code, your friend needs a blank graph like the one you started with.

They should read your code, mark the dots, and connect each one to the next with a line.

Set a challenge for a friend, or get two or more friends to race each other.

54

Game science

Graphs are useful for showing measurements and for sending coded information. In fact, screens on tablets and phones work in a similar way. The computer uses coordinates to figure out where you're touching the screen, and where to show pictures and text.

GRAPH MESSAGES

For another game challenge, can you use a graph to send a secret written message?

1 Figure out how to write letters using coordinates. Use a separate group of coordinates for each letter in your message.

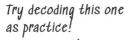
Try decoding this one as practice!

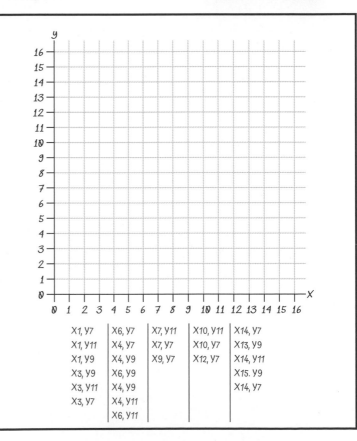

X1, Y7	X6, Y7	X7, Y11	X10, Y11	X14, Y7
X1, Y11	X4, Y7	X7, Y7	X10, Y7	X13, Y9
X1, Y9	X4, Y9	X9, Y7	X12, Y7	X14, Y11
X3, Y9	X6, Y9			X15. Y9
X3, Y11	X4, Y9			X14, Y7
X3, Y7	X4, Y11			
	X6, Y11			

HOW MANY TRIANGLES?

Time for something a little simpler. All you have to do is count the triangles!
What could be easier?

How to play

1 How many triangles can you see in this picture?

Did you get them all?
ARE YOU SURE?

Play these games on your own, or race against friends or family members.

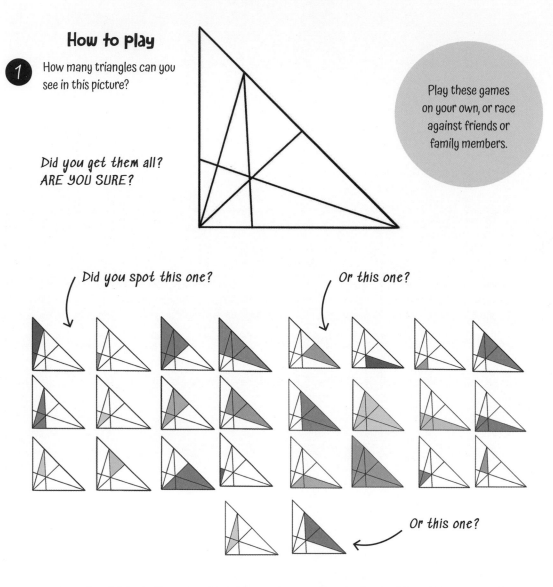

Did you spot this one?

Or this one?

Or this one?

In fact, though it looks like a very simple picture, there are lots of triangles hidden in here—26 of them in total. But it can be really hard to spot them all and keep track of them while you're counting.

HOW MANY TRIANGLES IN THE SQUARE?

1 Now that you know what to look for, try counting the triangles in this square. If it's tricky, you could try drawing lots of little copies of the square, then marking out the different triangles.

Try this, too!
Now try drawing your own triangle-filled shape to challenge a friend!

HOW MANY TRIANGLES IN THE STAR?

1 For the ultimate challenge, try counting the triangles in the star.

Ha ha ha!

SHAPE HUNT

Think you can spot a shape anywhere?
Time to test your brain!

Play on your own or
with friends.

How to play

 1 All you have to do in this game is find the
shapes that are trying to hide.

 3 Did you find them all? Try this one. You're
looking for a rectangle, a diamond, and a
perfect pentagon.

 2 Take a look at this tangled web and see if
you can spot them. There are two squares,
a hexagon (six-sided shape), and a star
somewhere in there!

I think
I'm lost!

Game science

It's hard for your brain to separate the outline of a shape
from the other lines all over it. However, some people are
better at this than others. This kind of game is sometimes
used as a test to find out how analytical people are. If you
have a very analytical brain, it means you're good at picking
out and understanding pictures, patterns, and rules.

THE MISSING PIECE

This game is the other way around!

 Here, you have a pattern with a piece missing.

Quick as you can, find the piece that will fit and complete the pattern. Which one is it?

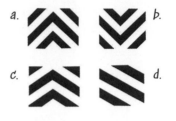

a.   b.

c.   d.

 Here's another one to try.

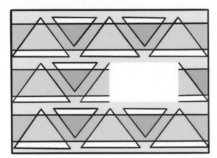

a.   b.

c.   d.

 It gets even harder if the pieces are not all the right way up!

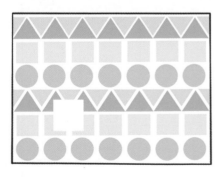

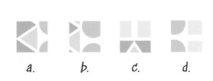

a.   b.   c.   d.

THE FEWEST SQUARES

Here's another game to play on graph paper. It might seem simple, but you could find yourself still puzzling over it several hours later!

How to play

 Draw a rectangular box on your graph paper using a pen or pencil and a ruler. It can be any size, but let's start with an easy one—a rectangle that's six squares wide and four squares high.

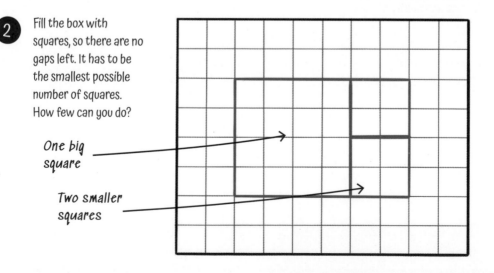

What do you need?
- Graph paper
- Pen or pencil
- Ruler

You can do this on your own, work together with a friend, or challenge each other to a contest.

2 Fill the box with squares, so there are no gaps left. It has to be the smallest possible number of squares. How few can you do?

One big square

Two smaller squares

A rectangle eight squares wide and five squares high

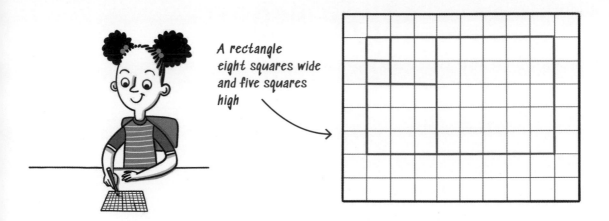

A rectangle 13 squares wide and 11 squares high

Game science

Is your brain aching yet? As you've probably discovered, you can spend ages trying out different solutions! It's actually very hard to be sure if you really have used the fewest squares possible, since there are so many variations—and the bigger the box you start with, the more there are!

If you're playing alone, try to use as few squares as possible. If you're playing against someone, the winner is the one who can use the fewest squares.

PAPER PEOPLE

Make a little row of people using just paper, a pencil, and scissors.
Once you start, you can't stop! (Until you run out of paper, that is ...)

How to play

1 Cut a long strip of paper—but not TOO long, since you need to fold it up and cut through it. A good size is about 30–50 cm (12–20 in) long and 10 cm (4 in) high.

2 Fold your paper strip neatly in a zigzag pattern, like this. Make each section roughly square or slightly narrower.

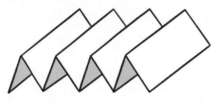

3 Press the folded strip flat, with the folded edges at the sides.

4 Now draw a person on it, with their arms and legs sticking out and touching the folded edges.

5 Finally, hold the folded paper firmly and cut around the shape through all the layers. Then, open out your chain of people.

Ta-daaa!

Game science

It doesn't have to be people—you can draw any shape you like. Dogs, dinosaurs, flowers, aliens, fairies, cars—whatever you draw will make a chain, as long as it touches the sides.

PAPER CIRCLE PATTERNS

This works in the same way, but instead of a strip, you start with a circle.

 1   Cut out a circle of paper roughly 20-40 cm (8-16 in) across. (Draw around a plate or pan lid to make it neat!)

 2   Now fold it in half, then in half again, then again, so it's folded into eight sections.

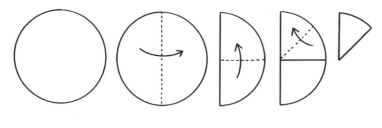

 3   Draw a picture or design on the folded paper, making sure it links at the sides ...

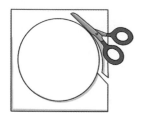

4   ... and open it out!

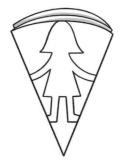

LOOPTURNER

Take some graph paper, think up a row of numbers,
and turn it into a super-loopy drawing!

How to play

There are many variations of this game, but let's do a simple three-number Loopturner to start with.

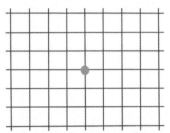

1 Draw a dot on the paper, somewhere near the middle.

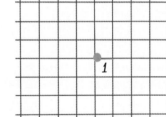

What do you need?

- Graph paper
- Pen or pencil

2 Now choose three numbers under 10. For example: 1, 3, 5.

3 Starting from your dot, draw a line one square long.

4 Turn a quarter-turn counterclockwise, and draw a line three squares long.

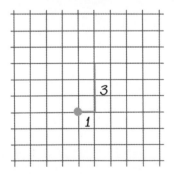

5 Turn a quarter-turn counterclockwise again, and—you guessed it!—draw a line five squares long.

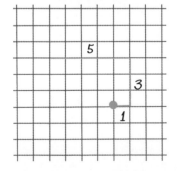

6 Now turn another quarter-turn counterclockwise, and repeat the pattern.

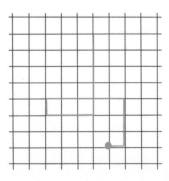

7 Keep drawing a one-square line, a three-square line, and a five-square line, turning the same way between each one, until you get back to where you started!

Amuse yourself for hours, or play with friends and set Loopturner challenges for each other.

Now try making some changes, and see what you get.

8 Try different arrangements of three numbers.

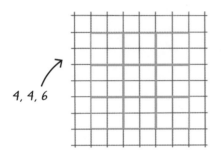

4, 4, 6

9 What about more numbers? It works with 4, 5, 6, or even more numbers—but you might not get the same type of pattern! In fact, some will go on forever instead of coming back to where you started ...

(Don't worry if your lines go over each other—just keep drawing!)

Game science

A loopturner is a little bit like a tiny computer program. Each row of numbers works like a "code" for a particular pattern. The patterns look complicated, yet they can be boiled down to just a short row of numbers and one simple instruction. Computer code often works in a similar way.

SNAKE

All you need for these games is a pen and some paper. For the first one, take turns making the snake grow longer and longer ...

Set it up

1 Draw a grid of dots, five high and five across, like this.

What do you need?

- Paper
- Pen

How to play

2 The players take turns adding a line to the grid to make the snake.

This is a game for two players (though you could try it with more).

3 There are just a few rules:

- Each line must be a straight line between two dots and must add to the existing snake.
- They must be horizontal, vertical, or a 45° diagonal, as shown here.
- The snake cannot cross over itself.
- You can't use the same dot twice.

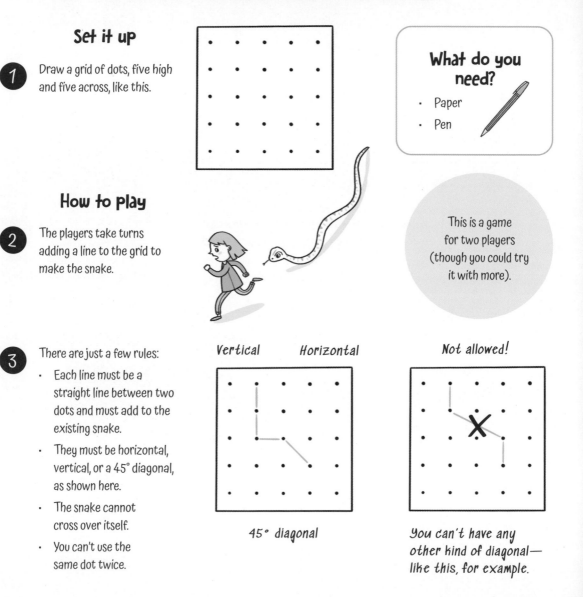

Vertical   Horizontal

Not allowed!

45° diagonal

You can't have any other kind of diagonal—like this, for example.

4 Keep adding lines to the snake (at either end). Eventually, it will be impossible to add anymore. The player who drew the last line is the loser!

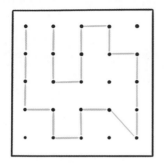

Game science

The snake always has to end, because you'll run out of space and dots. But with practice, you can use clever moves to trap your opponent into drawing the last line!

SNAKE BATTLE

One snake not enough for you? Try two!

1 Draw a 5 x 5 dot grid, the same as before. This time, both players have a pen in a different shade, and they each have their own starting points on the grid.

2 The players take turns drawing lines to make their own snakes.

- Each turn, they must draw a horizontal, vertical, or 45° diagonal line one square long.

- They must keep adding to the same end of the snake.

- The two snakes cannot cross or touch themselves or each other.

- You can't use the same dot twice.

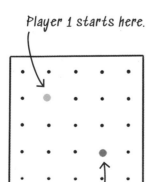

Player 1 starts here.

Player 2 starts here.

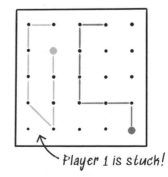

Player 1 is stuck!

Eventually, one player will be unable to move. They lose!

CHOMP

Be careful playing this game.
You don't want to have to chomp the rotten cake!

Set it up

1 Draw a grid of cakes or simple circles on a piece of paper, with a box around them, like this. This is your tray of cakes. It can be any size—ours is 4 x 6.

Lots of tasty cakes →

This is the → rotten cake!

What do you need?

- Paper
- Pen or pencil

Perfect for two players.

How to play

2 The players take turns playing. When it's your turn, choose a cake from the grid to chomp.

3 However, you don't just chomp that cake, but also all the cakes above it and to the right of it.

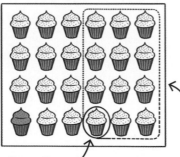

So if you choose this cake ...

... you must also chomp all these.

Game science

Mathematicians still haven't cracked the best way to play this game. See if you can figure out how to win!

Yuck!

4 Chomp your cakes by crossing or scribbling them out. Each player keeps doing this, until someone is forced to chomp the rotten cake!

SPROUTS

Next, try your hand at the simple, yet strange game of Sprouts ...

How to play

1 Start by drawing two dots on a piece of paper.

2 The two players use different pens, such as red and blue, and take turns adding lines.

3 When it's your turn, draw a line connecting two dots.

4 Then draw a new dot somewhere along your line. There are a few rules.

- Your line cannot cross itself or any other line.
- Each dot can have up to three lines joined to it. If a dot has three lines already, you can't add more.
- You can draw a line that starts at one dot and comes back to the same dot. However, this counts as two lines joining that dot, not one.

5 Keep playing until one player can't move and loses the game.

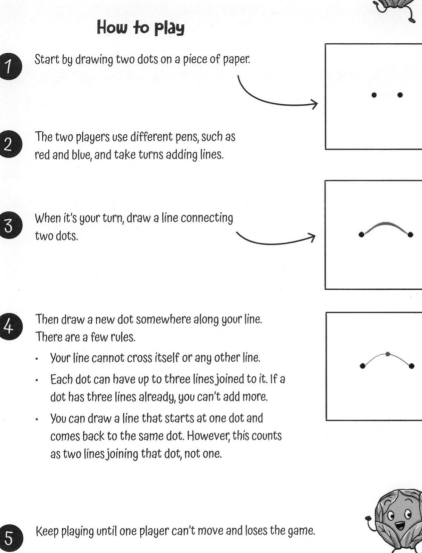

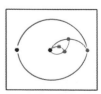
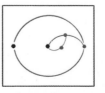

MAKE TRIANGLES

This simple game is fun to play, and you end up with a beautiful drawing, too.

How to play

 Start by drawing about 20 dots randomly all over the paper, fairly evenly spaced apart.

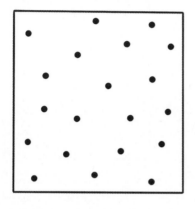

What do you need?

- Piece of paper
- Different shade of pen or crayon per person

This works well for two players, but you could also try it with three or more.

 The players take turns playing. At each turn, a player must add a straight line connecting two dots, using their own pen, like this.

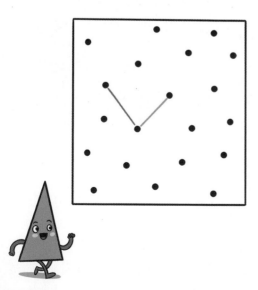

 The aim is to use your lines to make complete triangles.

It doesn't matter if you didn't draw all the lines in the triangle—you just have to be the one to complete it.

Whenever you make a triangle, you can fill it in with your own pen. The triangles cannot overlap or have a dot inside.

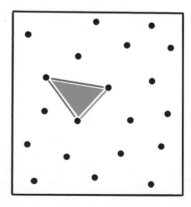

Keep taking turns and adding lines, trying to make as many triangles as you can. When all the dots are used up, count the triangles—the person with the most wins!

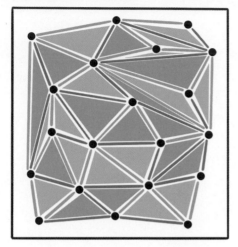

Come on, orange!

Game science

This is harder than it looks! Try not to give away triangles to your opponent by leaving two sides of a triangle for them to finish.

MAKE SQUARES

This game works the same way as the triangles game, but instead of making triangles, you try to make squares between the dots—or other four-sided shapes!

 As in Make Triangles, draw lots of dots, then take turns joining the dots with straight lines. This time, make four-sided or square shapes instead of triangles. When you make one, fill it in using your pen.

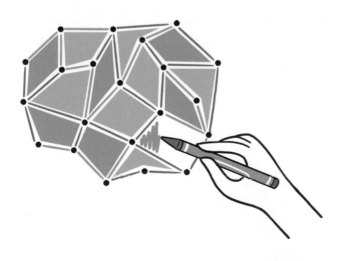

Sometimes, you'll find that your four-sided shape looks less like a square and more like an arrow.

BEWARE OF TRIANGLES!

Our last game was all about making triangles. Here's a game where you have to try NOT to make a triangle!

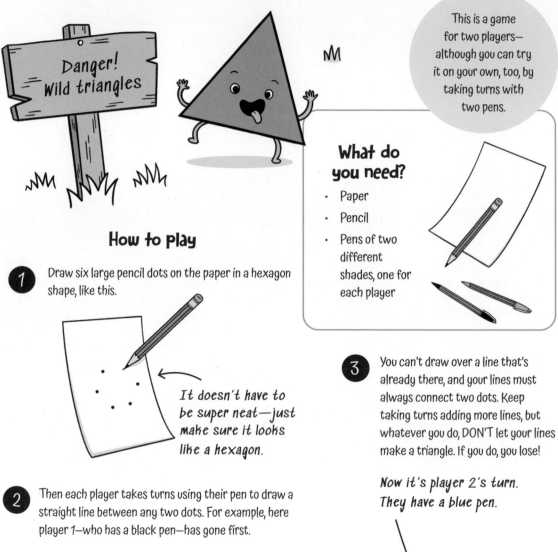

Danger! Wild triangles

This is a game for two players—although you can try it on your own, too, by taking turns with two pens.

What do you need?

- Paper
- Pencil
- Pens of two different shades, one for each player

How to play

1 Draw six large pencil dots on the paper in a hexagon shape, like this.

It doesn't have to be super neat—just make sure it looks like a hexagon.

3 You can't draw over a line that's already there, and your lines must always connect two dots. Keep taking turns adding more lines, but whatever you do, DON'T let your lines make a triangle. If you do, you lose!

Now it's player 2's turn. They have a blue pen.

2 Then each player takes turns using their pen to draw a straight line between any two dots. For example, here player 1—who has a black pen—has gone first.

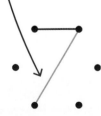

REMEMBER ...

If a triangle has been partly drawn by both players, no one loses. So, for example, this triangle is okay.

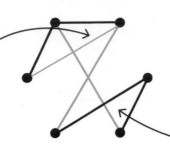

It's also okay if a triangle appears inside the hexagon and doesn't have a dot at all three corners, like this.

How long can you keep the game going?

It's all over ...

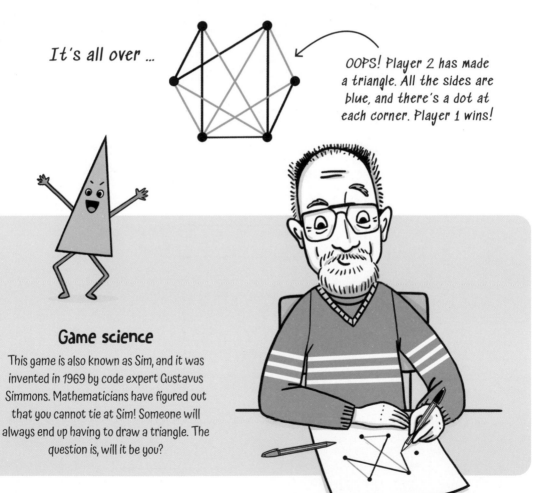

OOPS! Player 2 has made a triangle. All the sides are blue, and there's a dot at each corner. Player 1 wins!

Game science

This game is also known as Sim, and it was invented in 1969 by code expert Gustavus Simmons. Mathematicians have figured out that you cannot tie at Sim! Someone will always end up having to draw a triangle. The question is, will it be you?

DOT OF DOOM

Where will the dot of doom end up—and can you avoid it?

A game for two players.

How to play

1 On a piece of paper, draw a triangle made of 15 circles, like this.

2 You need two different pens, such as red and black, and each player uses their own.

What do you need?
- Paper
- Pens in different shades

3 To play, take turns writing the numbers 1–7 in the circles in order.

Player 1 writes a 1 in one of the circles.
Player 2 writes a 1 in another circle.
Player 1 writes a 2.
Player 2 writes a 2 ... and so on.

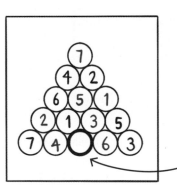

4 When both players have added the numbers 1–7, one circle will still be empty.

This is the DOT of DOOM!

5 The dot of doom destroys all the dots that touch it. Fill in the dot of doom and all the dots around it with a pen.

6 Count up the remaining numbers for each person. Whoever scores the highest is the winner!

Black WINS!

Game science
You don't want to put your highest numbers next to the dot of doom, but that's tricky, since you write the highest numbers last. Can you figure out the best strategy?

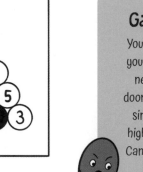

BALLOON POPPER

The aim of this game is simple—pop as many balloons as you can to win.

Best for two players.

 1 Draw a bunch of balloons on a piece of paper.

 3 On your next turn, you pop that balloon by filling it in, then draw a new dot on a balloon that is touching the first one.

4 Keep taking turns doing this—popping the balloon you drew a dot on, then drawing a new dot next to it.

2 Each player uses a different shade of pen to play. First, each person draws a dot on a balloon they plan to pop.

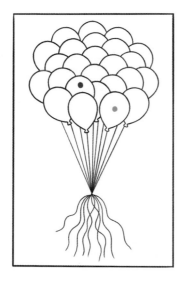

POP!

The loser is the first person who has nowhere to draw a new dot!

BLOCKS

Draw a 0 or an X, and block your opponent!

Set it up

 Draw a grid on a piece of paper, making it six squares across and six squares high. (Or just draw a box on squared or graph paper, if you have some.)

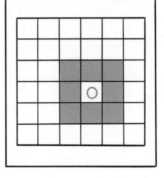

You need two players for this game.

How to play

 The players choose Os or Xs, the same as in a game of tic-tac-toe (see page 82), then take turns playing.

 When it's your turn, choose a square and draw your symbol in it. Then use the pencil to lightly shade in all the squares around it to make a "block."

What do you need?

- Paper
- Ruler
- Marker or pencil

4 The other player cannot put their symbol anywhere in your block. They have to choose an empty square. However, their block squares can overlap yours.

So they might do this, for example.

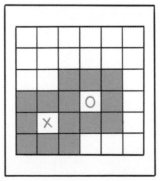

5 Keep taking turns adding your symbols and blocks.

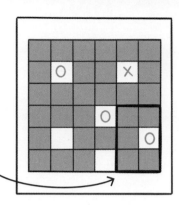

You are allowed to put a symbol in a square at the edge, like this.

Game science

The more you overlap the other player's blocks, the more space you leave free for the next move. The farther away from them you go, the more spaces you'll fill up with your block! You can use either of these sneaky strategies, depending on the stage of the game and whether you want to save space or use it up.

6 But eventually, there will be nowhere left to go. The first player who can't make a move loses the game.

You can find shape grids like these on the internet.

Try this too!

This game can be played on any size grid. Try a 10 x 10 or even a 20 x 20 grid.

You could also try using different types of grids, such as a grid of triangles or a grid of hexagons. Does the game work with them?

MOONS AND STARS

This game is easy to play but can keep you entertained for hours! You can draw moons and stars, hearts and flowers, dogs and cats, or whatever else you like in the boxes.

How to play

 First, draw a 6 x 6 grid of dots on paper (or it can be bigger if you like).

A game for two players.

What do you need?
- Paper
- Two pens or pencils in different shades (one for each player)

2 Decide who will be moons and who will be stars. Then take turns adding to the grid using different pens.

3 On your turn, draw one straight horizontal or vertical line between two dots.

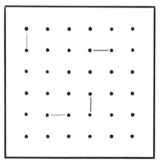

4 Your aim is to draw lines that complete square boxes. Whenever you do this, you win that square and draw your symbol inside it.

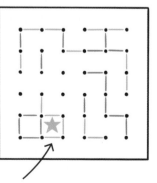

Green (stars) has completed this box and drawn a star inside.

5 Every time you complete a box, you get another turn. Sometimes, completing a box means that you can complete another box, and so on, so you get to claim a whole row of squares.

6 When you've filled up all the boxes, count them up and see who has the most.

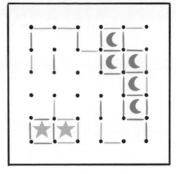

JOIN 5

Another dotty game to try!

You can play on your own, or two players can take turns.

How to play

1 This time, draw a grid of dots in a cross shape.

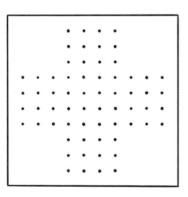

Start with a 4 × 4 grid in the middle. Add a 4 × 3 grid on each side.

2 To play a turn, draw a straight line, five dots long. It can be horizontal, vertical, or diagonal. It can link five existing dots, or you can use four existing dots and add a fifth dot (lined up with the others in the grid). Lines can meet or cross over each other, but they can't trace along each other.

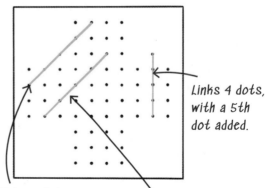

Links 4 dots, with a 5th dot added.

Links 5 existing dots.

Links 4 dots, with a 5th dot added.

3 Keep adding lines until you can't do any more! How many can you fit in?

NUMBER MAZES

Find your way through a maze made of numbers instead of walls!

You can solve these mazes on your own or with someone else. When you're good at it, create new mazes for friends or family to solve.

How to play

1 Here's your first challenge—a simple number maze. As with any maze, you begin at the start line and try and make your way through to your destination. To get there, you have to follow a path made up of numbers in order, from 1–20.

What do you need?
- Paper
- Pencil
- Ruler

START HERE

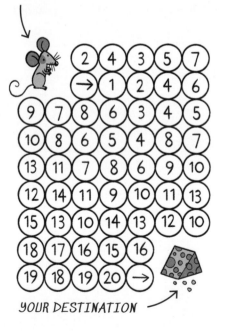

YOUR DESTINATION

2 This works the same way, but you're following the three times table.

START HERE

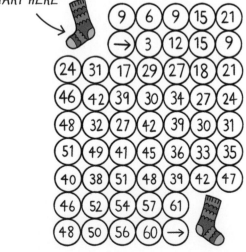

3 What about this one? You can only land on even numbers to get through the maze.

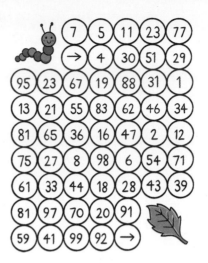

Game science

These mazes are similar to the number sequence games on page 28, but instead of finding the missing number, you have to pick out the sequence or route from the random numbers it's hiding among.

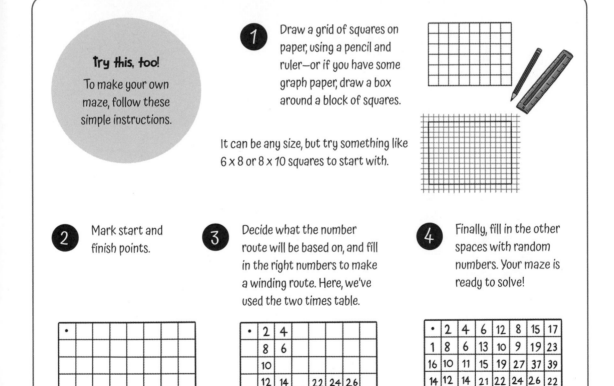

Try this, too!
To make your own maze, follow these simple instructions.

1 Draw a grid of squares on paper, using a pencil and ruler—or if you have some graph paper, draw a box around a block of squares.

It can be any size, but try something like 6 x 8 or 8 x 10 squares to start with.

2 Mark start and finish points.

3 Decide what the number route will be based on, and fill in the right numbers to make a winding route. Here, we've used the two times table.

4 Finally, fill in the other spaces with random numbers. Your maze is ready to solve!

TIC-TAC-TOE

Also known as noughts and crosses or Xs and Os,
this is a classic, super-simple game.

A two-player game.

How to play

1 Draw a simple 3 x 3 grid on paper, like this ...

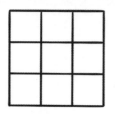

... or like this.

2 The players choose Os or Xs, then take turns drawing their symbol on the grid. First to get three symbols in a straight line wins!

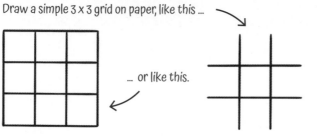

O wins!

Game science

Remember to try and stop your opponent from getting three in a row, too. The possible rows of three often pass through the middle square. So if you get to go first, always go in the middle!

TIC-TAC-TOE 4S

What happens if you make tic-tac-toe bigger?

1 For this game, draw a 4 x 4 grid on paper.

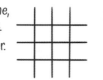

2 As in normal tic-tac-toe, players choose O or X and take turns filling in a square—but you try to get four in a row instead of three.

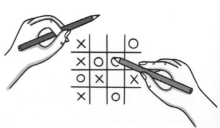

MULTI TIC-TAC-TOE
The ultimate tic-tac-toe!

 1 First, draw your grid, which should look like this:

A large tic-tac-toe grid ... with a small tic-tac-toe grid in each square

2 The first player draws their symbol in any of the squares.

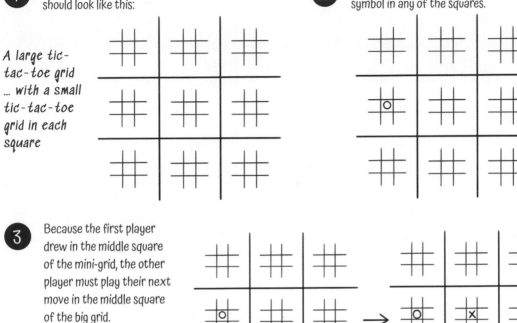

3 Because the first player drew in the middle square of the mini-grid, the other player must play their next move in the middle square of the big grid.

4 This happens each turn. Whichever square in the mini-grid a player draws in, that decides which square in the big grid the other player must use next.

 5 When one player wins a mini-grid, they draw their symbol on it. (If it's a draw, scribble it out).

6 If the previous move tells you to play on a completed grid, you can choose any other grid instead.

7 By winning the mini-grid games, try and win the big game!

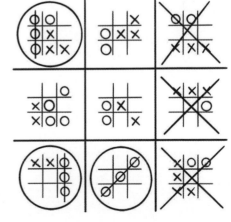

 X wins!

BATTLESHIPS

Shoot at your opponent's ships, and see how many you can sink.

For two players.

Set it up

1 Draw your game grids, using graph paper if possible. Each player needs a piece of paper with two grids on it, side by side. They should look like this:

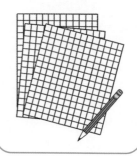

What do you need?

- Paper, ideally graph paper
- Pen or pencil

2 Set the game up so that the players can't see each other's grids. For example, you could sit opposite each other at a table, with a cereal box between you.

3 Each player now draws five boats on their first grid, in random places.

1 battleship: 4 squares

1 cruiser: 3 squares

1 submarine: 2 squares

2 tugs: 1 square each

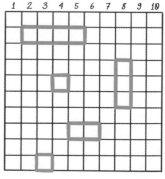

How to play

4 To play a turn, you "shoot" at a square on your opponent's grid by saying its name, such as "F5." They tell you whether it's a hit and has landed on one of their boats, or a miss (which has landed in the sea!).

5 Keep track of your results on your second grid. If it's a hit, put an X in square F5. If it's a miss, put a O.

Square F5.
It's a hit!

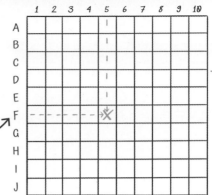

6 Then, the other player aims at one of your squares. Tell them if they hit or missed, and mark an X or O on your first grid—an X for where they hit a boat, and an O where they missed.

7 Keep taking turns, and the grids will start to fill up with Os and Xs.

8 When a player has hit all the squares on an opponent's boat, they've sunk it! The first to sink all their opponent's boats is the winner.

Your four-square battleship is the pride of your fleet. If your opponent sinks it, you shout:

You sank my battleship!

ROLLERBALL

This simple target game combines aiming and numbers skills.

What do you need?

- Large cardboard box
- Scissors
- Markers
- A pile of books
- Some marbles (or other small, heavy balls)
- A flat, smooth surface, like a hard floor, to play on
- A cardboard tube (the longer the better)

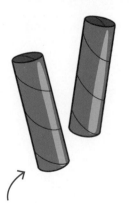

↑

You could use a tube from a roll of paper towel, foil, or food wrap, or a longer tube from a roll of wrapping paper.

Set it up

 1 With an adult to help, cut the flaps off the top of the cardboard box (don't throw them away).

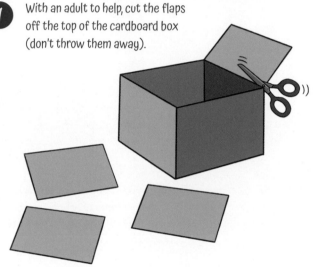

 2 Turn the box over, and mark a row of six tunnel shapes along the bottom.

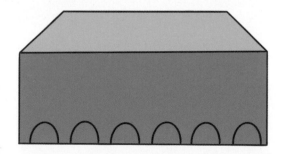

3 Carefully cut out the shapes to make six holes, and mark them with the numbers 5, 20, 50, 30, 15, and 5.

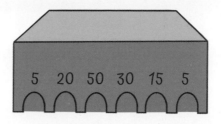

4 Now take your cardboard tube and lean it on a pile of books, so that it slopes gently downhill. Put the target box about 1–2 m (3–6 ft) away, and you're ready to roll!

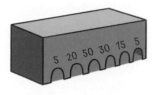

How to play

5 To play, aim the tube at the target, and roll a ball down the tube toward it.

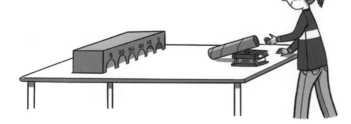

This can be played by any number of people.

You have to get 75!

- Give yourself a number of shots, such as three or five, and try and get the highest possible total. Play on your own, or take turns with other players to see who can get the highest score.

- Choose a multiple of 5 between 15 and 100, and challenge the other players to get that exact score.

For example, to do this, you have to score a combination of different numbers that add up to 75—such as 50, 15, and 10.

AIM AND FIRE!

This target game is slightly harder than the last one, because you have to fire
your ball through the air, not just along the ground!

Set it up

1 Attach the middle of
the spoon handle to
the pencil or chopstick
by looping a rubber
band around them
several times.

Any number
of people can play.

2 Push the ends of the
pencil or chopstick
through the sides of
the box. Ask an adult
to help you make
holes in the box first
if this is tricky.

What do you need?

- Smallish box
- Medium-sized spoon
- Pencil or chopstick
- Scissors
- Rubber bands
- A paper clip
- Tape
- Harmless missiles, such as
  cotton balls, mini pom-poms, or
  balls of crumpled paper
- Boxes or bowls to use as
  targets

3 Tie one end of a rubber
band to the end of the
spoon handle. With an
adult's help, use a pencil
or sharp scissors to
make a hole in the base
of the box. Thread
the other end of the
rubber band through
the hole.

Loop the paper clip through
the rubber band, and tape it
in place.

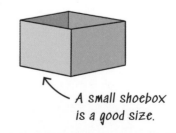

A small shoebox
is a good size.

How to play

4 Now you should be able to press down on the spoon and let it go, making it flip back up!

5 Now you just need some targets, such as small plastic food containers, paper bowls, or cardboard boxes. Label them with different scores, such as 10, 20, 50, and 100, and stand them 2–3 m (3–10 ft) away from your shooter. Put the high-scoring targets farther away!

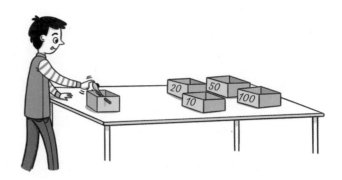

6 To play, put a missile in the bowl of the spoon, aim, and fire! How many can you score?

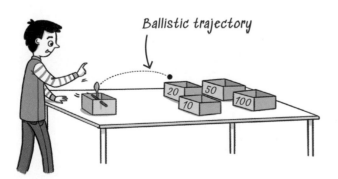

Ballistic trajectory

Game science

This game involves a kind of mathematics called ballistics. You have to calculate how far to pull the spoon down to make the missile fly the right distance and hit the target. As it flies, it will sail through the air in a curve called the ballistic trajectory.

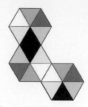

HEXTILES

This game is kind of like dominoes, but with hexagons!

Set it up

1 First, make your hexagon tiles. You need about 20–30 tiles, or more if you like. Start by tracing this hexagon template onto tracing paper or parchment paper, using a pencil and ruler. Cut it out and use it to draw hexagons on your cardboard.

For 1–4 players or more if you have enough tiles.

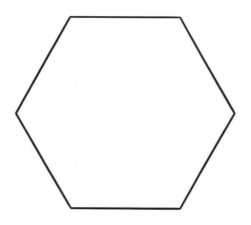

What do you need?

- Cardboard thin enough to cut easily. White craft cardboard is best, but a cereal box or other cardboard box will work, too
- Pencil
- Ruler
- Scissors
- Tracing paper or parchment paper
- Markers in different shades

2 Carefully cut out each hexagon tile. Then draw lines across the middle of each one, joining the corners, like this.

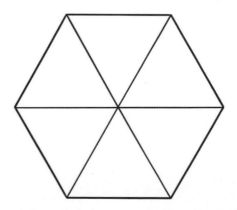

Now take your markers and use a different one to fill in each triangle.

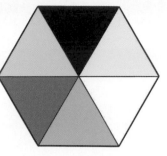

 Do this with all the hexagons. Each hexagon should have six different triangles—one of each shade—but it doesn't matter what order they're in. When you have 20 or more hexagons, you can start playing.

How to play

 Divide the hexagons equally between the players.

 Then take turns putting the tiles down on a flat surface.

If you match one triangle, you get one point. You get two points if you match two—and so on! When the tiles are all used up, the person with the highest score wins.

Each player must place their tile so that the triangles match, like this.

You might be able to match two triangles at once, like this.

TREASURE ISLAND

Set a trail of clues to reveal where the treasure is hidden.

Set a hidden treasure challenge for a friend—or you could both set one for each other.

What do you need?

- Graph paper
- Ruler
- Pens and pencils
- Crayons

Set it up

1 Start by marking out a map grid on your paper. Draw a large box about 15 cm (6 in) wide and 20 cm (8 in) high. If it's on graph paper, it will already have squares in it. If not, draw your own horizontal and vertical lines inside the box using a ruler, 1 cm (0.5 in) apart.

2 Mark the squares along the top with numbers 1 to 15, and the squares down one side with the letters A to T.

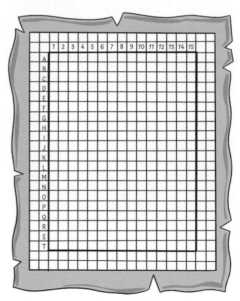

3 Now draw a map of a deserted treasure island on your grid. Add details, such as sandy bays, cliffs, mountains, a volcano, a forest, old ruins—whatever you like. Include a compass to show North, South, East, and West. You could add place names, too, if you like.

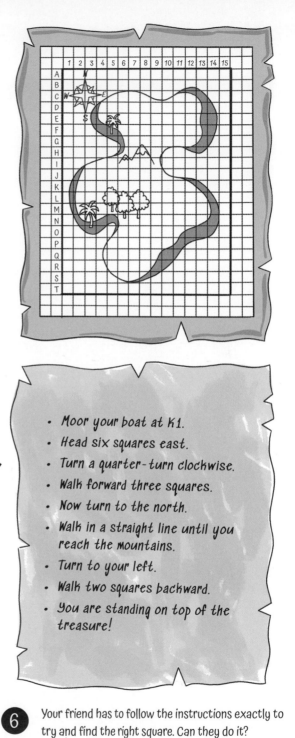

How to play

4 To play the game, decide which square makes the best hiding place for your pirate treasure. Don't mark it on the map, but write it down on a separate piece of paper as a coordinate—such as I9, for example.

5 Then write your friend a set of instructions for finding the treasure.

It could be something like this:

- Moor your boat at K1.
- Head six squares east.
- Turn a quarter-turn clockwise.
- Walk forward three squares.
- Now turn to the north.
- Walk in a straight line until you reach the mountains.
- Turn to your left.
- Walk two squares backward.
- You are standing on top of the treasure!

6 Your friend has to follow the instructions exactly to try and find the right square. Can they do it?

NUMBER SEQUENCE DOT-to-DOT

Make a mathematical dot-to-dot puzzle for a friend to solve.

Set it up

1 Before making your own, look at this one to see how it works.

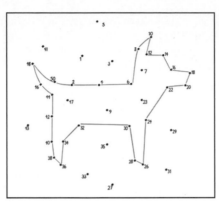

- Instead of just joining the dots, you have to find the numbers that make a sequence.

- In this puzzle, it's the even numbers from 2–50.

- So, first you find the number 2 and start there.

- Then you find 4 and draw a line to that— then 6, 8, 10, and so on.

What do you need?

- Paper
- Pencil

Set a challenge for a friend, or get two or more friends to race each other.

2 Decide what to use as your picture—a cat, for example.

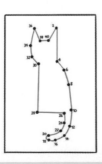

Using a pencil, lightly draw a simple cat on paper using a single line.

3 With the pen, draw dots along the line.

Put dots at the corners ...

... and along curved lines.

4 Number the dots with a number sequence. It could be even numbers, like the example above, or any other sequence.

5 Now erase your pencil drawing, leaving just the dots.

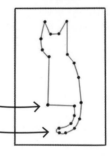

2 4 6 8 10 12 14 16 18 20 22 24

6 Finally, fill in the paper with other dots, and give them numbers, too—make sure you don't use any of the numbers from your sequence.

EXTRA TRICKY DOT-TO-DOT

Here's an even harder dot-to-dot challenge!

1 As in the previous game, lightly draw a simple picture using a pencil.

2 Use a pen to draw dots along the lines and at the corners.

3 Then add your numbers—but this time, make them completely random. For example, you might use these numbers.

•11 •25 •40 •19 •3 •100 •29 •77 [etc]

4 Before you erase the pencil lines, write down the numbers in the right order, like this.

11
25
40
19
3
100
29
77

7×11 $25 - 6$
5×5 $5 + 6$ $12 \div 4$
10×4 10×10

5 Now turn each number into an equation. For example, the first number is 11. You could make this into 6 + 5.

1. $6 + 5$
2. 5×5
3. 10×4
4. $25 - 6$
5. $12 \div 4$
6. 10×10
7. $5 + 16 + 8$
8. 7×11

6 Do this for all the numbers, then erase your pencil lines, and add more dots to the picture. Give them random numbers that are not the ones you've already used.

Can a friend solve your puzzle?

3D TIC-TAC-TOE

You can play tic-tac-toe—but can you play it in three dimensions?

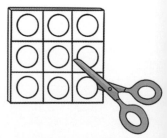

This game is for two players.

Set it up

 Draw six squares on the cardboard, using a pen and a ruler. Make them about 12 cm (5 in) long and wide. Carefully cut them out with an adult's help.

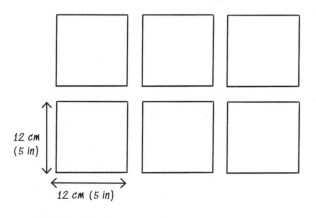

12 cm (5 in)

12 cm (5 in)

What do you need?

- Corrugated cardboard box
- Ruler
- Scissors
- Glue
- Four pencils or chopsticks
- Some red and black markers

2 On three of the squares, draw a nine-square grid.

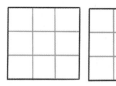

3 Then draw circles inside all the squares. You could draw around a coin to make it easier.

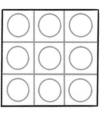

4 Ask an adult to help you cut out the circles using sharp scissors.

Take the three blank cardboard squares and glue them together in a stack.

 Then take one of the squares with holes in it and glue that on top.

 Now push the four pencils or chopsticks through the corners of one of the other two squares.

 Then push them through the other single square.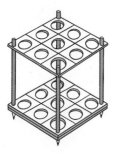

 Finally, push them into the stack of squares.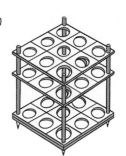

 Arrange the squares so that one is halfway up the pencils and the other is at the top.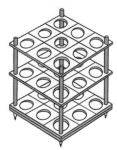

How to play

To make pieces, cut 15 circles and 15 crosses out of cardboard, and use marker pens to make the Xs red and the Os black.

To play, the two players take turns placing their symbols on the squares, just like normal tic-tac-toe. But there are lots more ways to get three in a row!

You could have three in a row on any of the levels

... or a column of three on top of each other

... or a diagonal row of three from top to bottom.

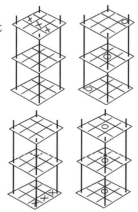

PONG HAU K'I

This traditional game from China could be the simplest mathematical game of all.

How to play

 1 Draw a line about 12 cm (5 in) long on your paper. Add two more lines the same length to make three sides of a square.

 2 Add two diagonal lines across the middle. Then add dots at all the corners.

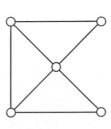

3 For the pieces, use buttons, counters from another game, or just make them from paper.

4 Put the counters in the starting position, like this:

Each player picks a shade.

This is a two-player game.

What do you need?

- Paper
- Pencil
- Ruler
- Four playing pieces, two of one shade and two of another

5 On each turn, you must move one of your counters along one line to the empty dot. (You can't go past a dot or jump over another counter.)

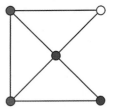

6 Keep taking turns until one player is stuck and can't move.

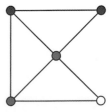

Game science

It's possible to keep playing this game forever without anyone winning. But if you make a mistake, you'll end up stuck.

HAWAIIAN LU-LU

This fun game uses four special counters, and depends totally on luck!

Set it up

1 Draw around the coin onto the cardboard eight times, then cut out the circles to make eight pieces. Glue them together in pairs to make four thicker counters.

Any number of people can play.

What do you need?

- Thick cardboard
- Pencil
- Scissors
- Glue
- Pen
- A large coin to draw around

2 On one side of each counter, draw these four patterns.

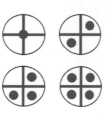

How to play

3 The players take turns throwing the counters. On your turn, you get two throws.

- If some counters land upside down on the first throw, pick those counters up and throw them again. Then count up how many dots you scored.

- If all your counters land the right way up, you score 10 and get a second throw. Add the scores from both throws together.

- Each player adds up their score as they go.

First to reach 100 wins!

SHISIMA

This game from Kenya is like a combination of Tic-tac-toe and Pong Hau K'i.

Set it up

1 Shisima is played on an octagon-shaped board, with eight lines leading into the middle, where there is a small lake. It looks like this:

This game is for two players.

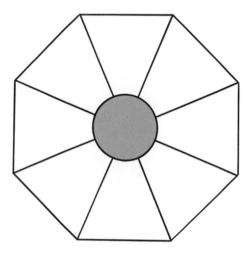

What do you need?

- Paper
- Pencil
- Ruler
- Pen
- Six counters, three of one shade and three of another

2 Use a ruler and pencil to copy the board onto paper, and shade in the lake. For counters, use buttons, counters from another game, or your own homemade counters made from cardboard or paper.

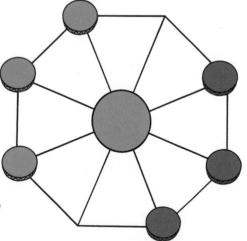

3 Set up the board with the counters opposite each other in rows of three.

How to play

4 Each player should pick one set of pieces. Decide who's going first, then take turns moving.

On each turn, you can move one of your pieces along one line to another corner or into the middle.

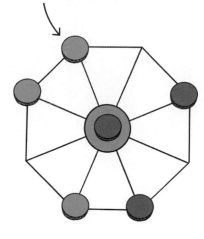

You can only move one space at a time, and you can't jump.

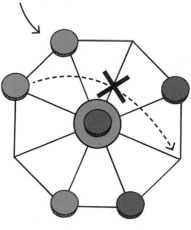

5 The winner is the first to get all their pieces in a straight line, with one of them in the middle.

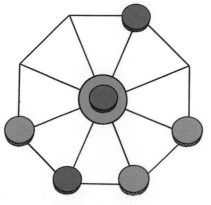

Game science

To win, you need one of your pieces in the middle. But if you move to the middle too early, you may get stuck and have to move out again, giving your opponent a chance to sneak in! Play a few times, and you'll start to figure out a winning strategy.

SOLITAIRE

Jump your pieces over each other until there's only one left.

This is a one-player game.

Set it up

1 Measure and cut out a piece of cardboard about 25 cm (10 in) square.

What do you need?

- Cardboard
- Scissors
- Pencil
- Ruler
- Markers
- 32 small coins, buttons, or game counters

2 In the middle of the cardboard, draw a smaller square that's about 17.5 cm (7 in) along each side.

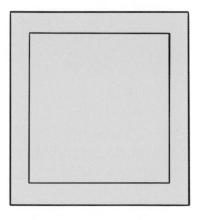

3 Divide the square into seven equal rows and seven equal columns by drawing pencil lines, like this. The lines should be about 2.5 cm (1 in) apart.

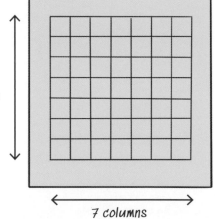

7 rows

7 columns

4 Now, using a marker, add dots in some of the boxes to make this pattern. Shade in the four blocks in each corner, since they are not part of the playing area.

5 There are 33 dots on the board, but you only have 32 pieces. Put a piece on each dot, apart from the dot in the middle. Now you're ready to play.

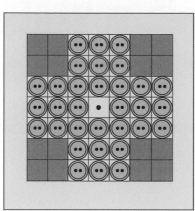

your board is ready!

How to play

6 To make a move, pick up a piece and make it jump over one of the pieces next to it, either horizontally or vertically, into an empty space. Then take the counter that was jumped over off the board.

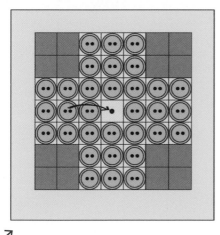

To start with, there's only one empty space, so you'll have to jump into that one. But as more and more pieces get removed, you'll have more choices.

7 The aim is to remove all the pieces from the board except one.

Game science

It sounds easy, but take care! If you don't watch out, you could end up leaving a piece stuck by itself far away from the others, so you can't jump over it.

SCYTALES

A scytale is an amazing device for making a secret coded message. It was invented in ancient Greece.

How to play

 Cut some long, narrow strips of paper about 1–2 cm (0.5 in) wide. One way to make a strip like this is to cut all the way down one side of a piece of printer paper.

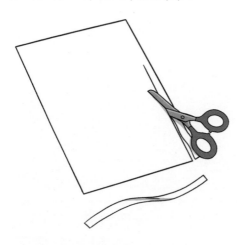

Use scytales to make coded messages for your friends or family to unscramble.

 To make your coded message, take a long, cylinder-shaped object—here it's a narrow tube from a roll of foil.

3 Tape the end of the strip of paper to one end of the cylinder.

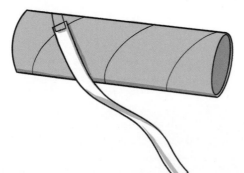

What do you need?

- Paper
- Scissors
- Tape
- Pen
- Cylinder-shaped objects, such as cardboard tubes
- A wooden spoon with a straight handle
- Pens and pencils, or a rolling pin.

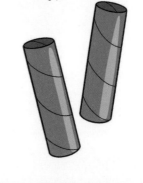

4 Then wrap the strip around the tube in a neat spiral.

5 Now you can write your secret spy message along the tube, putting a separate letter on each section of paper.

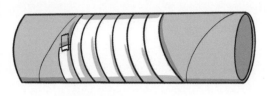

6 To scramble the message, carefully unwind it from the cylinder and fold it up neatly.

7 In this form, the letters on the strip are pretty much impossible to make sense of. The only way to read the message is to wrap the strip around the cylinder again—or another cylinder that's exactly the same width.

If you use the wrong size of cylinder, it won't work!

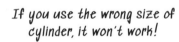

To send a message to someone far away like the Greeks did, you both need to have the same type of cylinder. You use yours to encode the message, and they use theirs to decode it.

8 You could give your friend several different sizes of cylinders, and challenge them to reveal the message by finding the one that works.

Athens this way! →

BUZZ

This game is fantastic for helping you remember your seven times table!

How to play

1 Everyone stands in a circle and takes turns throwing the ball or beanbag to someone else in the group. As you throw, you count up from one. So the first thrower shouts "one," the next thrower shouts "two," and so on. (It doesn't matter if someone drops the ball—just pick it up and keep going!)

What do you need?

- A small ball, like a tennis ball, or something else that's easy to throw and catch, such as a beanbag

- Space for everyone to stand in a big circle

This game is for any number of players from two upward.

BUZZ!

2 However, when you get to a number that's in the seven times table, you don't shout it out. Instead, you shout ... BUZZ!

3 If anyone forgets and says the number instead, everyone else shouts "BUZZ," and the person is out of the game.

Try this, too!

Of course, this will work with any times table. When you can do the seven times table perfectly, switch to another one, such as the five, eight, or 11 times table. And if that's too easy, try doing it backward starting at 100!

Times Tables

Need a quick reminder? These are the numbers in the seven times table.

1 2 3 4 5 6 7 8 9 10 11 12 13 14 15 16 17 18 19 20 21 22 23 24 25 26 27 28 29 30 31 32 33 34 35 36 37 38 39 40 41 42 43 44 45 46 47 48 49 50 51 52 53 54 55 56 57 58 59 60 61 62 63 64 65 66 67 68 69 70 71 72 73 74 75 76 77 78 79 80 81 82 83 84 85 86 87 88 89 90 91 92 93 94 95 96 97 98

MULTI-BUZZ

As you can probably tell, this game is similar to Buzz, but harder ...

1. This time, you're not going to just do one times table, but you'll do two at once. For example, you could try the seven times table and the 10 times table.
2. The rules are the same as for Buzz, but you shout "BUZZ!" when the number is in the seven times table OR the 10 times table.
3. What if it's in both, like the number 70? Then you shout "MULTI-BUZZ!"

BACK TO BACK

A split-second game of high-speed mathematics!

What do you need?

- A chalkboard or whiteboard (or you could tape some paper to the wall and write on that)
- Chalks or markers
- A calculator

This game works best with a large group of 20 people or more, such as your class! But you can play it with as few as three.

How to play

1. Choose two players to play against each other. They have to stand back to back, facing away from each other, in front of the wall or board. The rest of the group sit facing the board, so that they can see what's on it.

2. One person in the group is picked as the "caller." They shout out "Go!" and the two players have to quickly write a number on the wall next to them. They must stay facing away from each other, so they can't see the other person's number.

Now the caller must add up the two numbers or multiply them together. (They can use the calculator if it's hard.) They tell the players the answer.

OR

> The two numbers added together make 10!

> The two numbers multiplied together make 21!

4 Now the two players have to figure out the other player's number as fast as they can!

They know what their own number is, so they can figure it out.

> My number is 3
> 21 is 3 × 7 ...
> Theirs must be 7!

5 The winner is the first to shout out the other person's number. They get to stay at the front, while the loser swaps with someone new.

> Whoever can stay up at the front for the longest is the back-to-back champion!

GUESS MY NUMBER

Who will guess the secret number first?

99?
79?
21?

56?
34?

Set it up

1 For this game, you will need a big 10 x 10 grid listing all the numbers from 1–100. It could be drawn on a big piece of paper or on a whiteboard or chalkboard, or all the players could have their own smaller versions.

1	2	3	4	5	6	7	8	9	10
11	12	13	14	15	16	17	18	19	20
21	22	23	24	25	26	27	28	29	30
31	32	33	34	35	36	37	38	39	40
41	42	43	44	45	46	47	48	49	50
51	52	53	54	55	56	57	58	59	60
61	62	63	64	65	66	67	68	69	70
71	72	73	74	75	76	77	78	79	80
81	82	83	84	85	86	87	88	89	90
91	92	93	94	95	96	97	98	99	100

What do you need?

- Whiteboard, chalkboard, or large piece of paper
- Marker or pens—or if you are using a chalkboard, chalks!

This game is for five or more players.

How to play

2 One person is picked to be the chooser. Inside their head, they think of a number anywhere from 1–100.

3 Once they've chosen it, the other players take turns asking questions about the number. They could make a guess, such as:

Is it 45?

Or they could ask a more general question, like:

Is it in the 10 times table?

Is it an odd number?

Is it less than 30?

4 Each time, the chooser answers the question and then marks the grid to show which numbers it could or couldn't be. For example, imagine that the question is "Is it under 30?"

1	2	3	4	5	6	7	8	9	10
11	12	13	14	15	16	17	18	19	20
21	22	23	24	25	26	27	28	29	30
31	32	33	34	35	36	37	38	39	40
41	42	43	44	45	46	47	48	49	50
51	52	53	54	55	56	57	58	59	60
61	62	63	64	65	66	67	68	69	70
71	72	73	74	75	76	77	78	79	80
81	82	83	84	85	86	87	88	89	90
91	92	93	94	95	96	97	98	99	100

If the answer is no, the chooser crosses out all the numbers under 30.

5 What if the next question is "Is it in the 10 times table?" If the answer is yes, it must be 40, 50, 60, 70, 80, 90, or 100. So the chooser circles all these numbers.

1	2	3	4	5	6	7	8	9	10
11	12	13	14	15	16	17	18	19	20
21	22	23	24	25	26	27	28	29	(30)
31	32	33	34	35	36	37	38	39	(40)
41	42	43	44	45	46	47	48	49	(50)
51	52	53	54	55	56	57	58	59	(60)
61	62	63	64	65	66	67	68	69	(70)
71	72	73	74	75	76	77	78	79	(80)
81	82	83	84	85	86	87	88	89	(90)
91	92	93	94	95	96	97	98	99	(100)

6 Eventually, you'll narrow it down to just a few numbers, and it will get easier to guess. The first person to get it right becomes the chooser and picks the next number.

If each person has their own small grid, they do the crossing out or circling numbers themselves.

Try this, too!

You can play this without the grid—for example, riding in a car. It's much harder, though, because you have to try and remember all the questions and answers, and also which numbers it can and can't be.

COUNT TO 30

Count to 30? That sounds easy enough, right? Except in this game, you DON'T want to be the one who has to say "30!"

This is good for a group of between 10 and 20 players.

What do you need?

- A group of friends to play with
- Brainpower!

How to play

1 Everyone sits in a circle, and one person is chosen to start.

2 They start counting up from one, but they can choose to say just one number, or two or three numbers.

3 Keep going around the circle. Each person counts from the last number, but each time, they can choose whether to say one, two, or three numbers.

So the game might go like this:

Three ...

Four, five, six ...

Seven ...

Eight, nine ...

Ten, eleven, twelve ...

One, two ...

... and so on!

4 Whoever ends up having to say "30" is out. Keep playing until there are only two people left to battle it out!

SLOW ON THE DRAW

Can you fool your audience about which number you're drawing?

This is good for a class-sized group.

How to play

1 One person is picked to be the slow-on-the-draw number artist.

2 They choose a number from 0–9 and start drawing it on the board or paper as slowly and confusingly as possible, so that it's hard to tell what it is.

For example, you might start by drawing a half-circle, like this. →

This could be part of a 2, a 3, a 5, a 6, an 8, or a 9.

Slowly add a little more ...

It could still be a 6, an 8, or a 9. Or is it a 0 that's already finished?

What do you need?

- A chalkboard, a whiteboard, or a big piece of paper taped to the wall
- Chalk or a marker

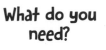

3 Keep slowly adding to your number.

4 The first person to shout out the right answer becomes the next to draw.

VENN GAME

This game is all about Venn diagrams—a handy way of putting things into groups, often used by mathematicians.

What is a Venn diagram?

A Venn diagram uses overlapping circles to sort out objects. Here's an example using numbers.

This Venn diagram has two overlapping circles.

This circle is for odd numbers up to 20.

This circle is for square numbers up to 20. (What are square numbers? See page 50!)

In the overlapping area, you put numbers that are both.

Numbers that don't go in any of these groups fall outside the diagram.

4   1   3   5   6   20
    16   9   7   11   10   2
        13   15   8   12
    17   19   14   18

This is great for large groups. For fewer people, try the tabletop version opposite.

What do you need?

- A large outdoor space, such as a playground or sports field
- Something to make circles with, such as chalk, ropes, mini flags, or cones

How to play

1   Make two large circles that overlap on the ground.

Label them A and B.

A   B

2 A caller shouts out what the two circles stand for:

"Circle A people love dogs!"

"Circle B people love cats!"

Here are some more ideas:

Circle A = likes broccoli
Circle B = likes tomatoes

Circle A = likes camping
Circle B = likes basketball

Circle A = has brown hair
Circle B = has glasses

3 On the count of three, everyone has to run to the right place. If you only like cats or dogs, you go to that circle. If you like both, you go in the overlapping area. If you don't like either, you stay outside!

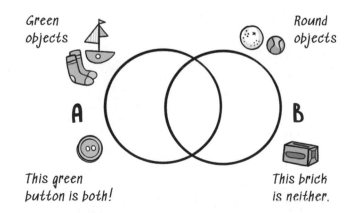

Try this, too!

Use loops of string to make two overlapping circles on a table. Write some adjectives on pieces of paper and put them in a container. Mix them up, then draw two of them. Now race to find some suitable objects!

Green objects

Round objects

A

B

This green button is both!

This brick is neither.

What have you found after one minute? Score one point for each object in a circle, and score five points for an object in the overlapping part of the Venn diagram.

SUPER BINGO

This game takes some preparation, so get it ready in advance.

> This is for groups of 5-10 people, plus a bingo caller. Each player will need their own bingo card.

Set it up

1 Draw and cut out a piece of cardboard about 12 cm (5 in) square for each player.

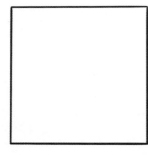

What do you need?

- Plain cardboard
- Scissors
- Ruler
- Pen and paper
- Cup
- A pencil for each player

2 On each card, draw a 3 x 3 grid of nine squares.

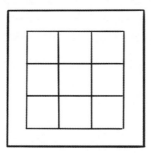

3 Write the numbers 1-20 on paper, and cut them up into separate numbers. Put them in a cup or pot, and shake them up.

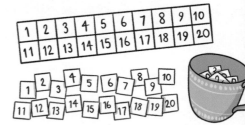

4 Pick nine numbers at random out of the cup. For example, you might pick these nine:

2	15	4
18	11	7
8	16	20

5 Copy them onto one of the cards like this:

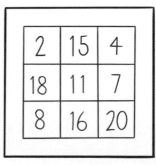

2	15	4
18	11	7
8	16	20

6 Keep doing the same thing to make all the cards—but for each new card, check to make sure that you haven't picked the exact same numbers that another card has. All the cards should have a different mix of numbers on them.

2	6	17
12	3	5
14	8	1

14	3	18
9	10	2
15	4	8

11	19	4
7	10	3
20	1	5

1	7	12
20	5	18
11	3	6

7 Next, write the numbers 1–20 in a list. Next to each number, write a mathematics problem that equals that number—like this:

1	10 – 9
2	4 ÷ 2
3	24 – 21
4	12 ÷ 3
5	2 + 3
6	36 ÷ 6
7	18 – 11
... and so on	

8 Cut up the list into separate mathematics problems.

10 – 9	36 ÷ 6
4 ÷ 2	2 + 3
24 – 21	18 – 1
12 ÷ 3	

 9 Then take the numbers out of the cup, and put all the mathematics problems in!

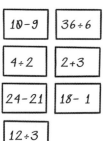

How to play

 10 Give each person a bingo card and a pen or pencil.

2	15	4
18	11	7
8	16	20

 11 The caller pulls a problem out of the cup at random and reads it out. (NOT the answer!)

24 – 21

 12 The players have to figure out the answer and check to see if it's on their card. If it is, they cross it off.

 13 The caller keeps doing this, and eventually, one player will have crossed off all the numbers on their card. They shout SUPER BINGO! and win the game!

Super Bingo!

BEETLE

This is a famous and fun mathematics game.
The aim is to be the first to draw the beetle!

How to play

 1 The players sit around a table or in a circle on the floor, and take turns playing.

2 When it's your turn, you roll the dice. Depending on what number you roll, you may be able to start drawing your beetle or add body parts to it.

 3 The different dice numbers stand for different parts of the beetle.

What do you need?

- Some paper and a pen or pencil for each player
- A dice, which everyone can share

1 = Body

2 = Head

3 = A leg (6 in total)

4 = An eye (2 in total)

5 = An antenna (feeler) (2 in total)

6 = Tail

Any number can play Beetle, but it's easier with 2–10 players.

4 You have to roll a one to start drawing, since you need a body before you can attach other parts to it. When you get a one, draw the body.

5 On your next turn, you might roll a three—meaning that you could add a leg.

6 You need to roll a two and draw a head before you can add the eyes or antennae.

What if you can't draw anything?

If you roll a number you can't use, you just have to wait until it's your turn again.

For example, if you roll a 4 before you get a 2, you can't draw anything, since your beetle doesn't have a head yet.

Or you might have a beetle that already has all 6 legs, so you can't draw any more.

If you roll a 3, you can't add another leg, so you just wait for your next turn.

101 OUT

This is a dice-based team game where you're trying to get to exactly 101—but no higher!

How to play

 1 Each team picks a scorekeeper, who keeps the score on paper.

 2 The teams take turns playing. On each turn, they choose one person to roll the dice and shout out the number they've rolled.

It's a 3!

What do you need?

Each team needs:

· A dice

· Some paper

· A pen or pencil

Any number of people can play as two teams. So, for example, if you have 20 people, play in two teams of 10.

3 Each time the dice is rolled, the team can choose whether to use that number or to multiply it by 10. So, for example, if you roll a 3, you can count it as a 3 or as a 30.

= 3   or   = 30

4 The aim is to add up all the numbers your team scores and try and get to 101—but no higher.

5 At the start of the game, you'll want to use the 10 x bigger scores to increase the total quickly. But as you get closer to 101, you'll need the smaller numbers!

Dice throw	Score	Total
🎲	50	50
🎲	20	70
🎲	6	76
🎲	10	86
🎲	10	96
🎲	1	97
🎲	1	100

 6 If you hit 101 exactly, your team wins instantly! But if you go over 101, your team loses instantly.

7 If you're getting close to 101, you risk going over it and losing. So each team has to decide if they want to stop and stick with their total—such as 97 or 100. If this happens, the team with the score closest to (but not over) 101 is the winner. If they both get the same score, it's a draw.

101 battle
Each game is very quick, so you might want to keep playing and keep a running score of how many games each team wins.

TEAM NUMBERS

Here is a super-simple, fun, and noisy high-speed number game for teams.

Set it up

 1 Divide 20 large pieces of cardboard into two sets of 10, and use marker pens to write the numbers 0-9 on each set. Make the numbers as big and clear as you can.

How to play

You need two teams with at least four players in each, plus a caller to shout out numbers—so a minimum of nine people.

2 Give each team a set of cards, and send them to sit in two separate groups.

3 To play a round, the caller thinks of a number and shouts it out. The first team to show that number by holding up the cards wins a point. Simple! So, for example, the caller might choose the number 472.

472!

4 The players in each team have to find the three cards with 4, 7, and 2 on them, and line up a row of three people, each holding a card. And, of course, they have to be in the right order from the point of view of the caller and the other team.

5 The number the caller chooses can have any number of digits, up to the number of people on each team—so that there will be enough people to hold up the cards. So if each team has four people, the numbers can be one, two, three, or four digits.

6 If there are more players in each team, the caller can use longer numbers.

7 However, since each team only has one of each number, the digits must all be different. For example, you can use 6,371, but not 6,333—since the teams only have one card with a 3 on it.

37

this is a silly number game that's perfect for mathematics parties!

Set it up

 1 Before you start, write a list of about 8–10 numbers, and decide on an activity that each number will stand for. The group can work together to come up with ideas.

10	Jump up and down
21	Turn around twice
3	Clap
15	Put your hands on your head
99	Shout out your own name
7	Sit on the floor
42	Be totally silent

Any number of players, plus a caller to shout out the numbers.

What do you need?
- Board or paper
- Wall
- Marker or pencil
- Tape

How to play

2 Write the list in large writing on the board or on paper stuck to the wall where everyone can see it.

3 Everyone stands in the space and waits for the caller to shout out a number from the list.

4 As soon as you hear the number, you have to do that thing.

10!

5 The last person to do it is out and has to wait at the side (or they can go and help the caller).

6 When there's only one person left, they're the winner!

Hurray!

37

Why is it called 37? Because that's the special number. If the caller shouts 37, you have to do ALL the actions!

Game science

When you first start playing, the game will be slower. You won't remember all the numbers and what they mean, so you'll have to check the list. But the more you play it, the faster you'll get!

GLOSSARY

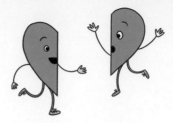

Average The middle or typical value of a group of numbers, found by adding the numbers together, then dividing by the number of numbers in the group.

Base ten A number system that uses ten digits, from 0 to 9.

Base two A number system that only uses two symbols—0 and 1.

Binary A counting system based on 2, instead of the usual base 10 (or decimal) system.

Circumference The distance around the edge of a circle.

Decimal number A number between two whole numbers, with part of the number written after a decimal point, such as 1.6 or 3.75.

Diameter The distance across the middle of a circle.

Digit A single whole number symbol. The digits we normally use in mathematics are 1, 2, 3, 4, 5, 6, 7, 8, 9, and 0. Digits are combined to make other, larger numbers.

Encryption The process of converting a message or other information into code.

Formula A rule or set of rules that can be applied to lead to a particular result.

Fraction A part of a number or amount, shown as a proportion of a whole. For example, three-quarters (¾) means three of four equal parts.

Hexagon A shape with six straight sides.

Horizontal A line or shape that runs from side to side, like the horizon.

Mathematician An expert in mathematics.

Pentagon A shape with five straight sides.

Pi A decimal number, roughly 3.141592, which is the result of dividing the circumference of any circle by its diameter.

Prime number A number that can only be divided by itself and 1, such as 17.

Proof A demonstration that shows that an idea or theory in mathematics is true.

Radius The distance from the middle to the edge of a circle.

Right angle An angle of 90°, such as the corner of a square.

Scytale A cylindrical tool used to send coded messages.

Semicircle A half-circle.

Sequence A series of numbers that follow a rule predicting what the next number will be.

Smoot A measurement of length equal to 1.702 m (5 ft 7 in), named after MIT student Oliver Smoot.

Square number A number that is another number multiplied by itself, such as 9 (which is 3 x 3). A square number of dots can be arranged in a square pattern.

Symmetrical A symmetrical shape that is the same on both sides—one side is a mirror image of the other.

Tangram A puzzle consisting of several smaller shapes that make up one large shape.

Tessellate A shape that can tessellate is one that tiles or fits together endlessly.

Venn diagram A type of diagram using overlapping circles to show how objects fit into different categories.

Vertical A line or shape that runs up and down, like a lamppost.

Whole number A complete number such as 3, 10, or 200, rather than a fraction or decimal number, such as 3 ½ or 3.5.

ANSWERS

P29: *1 2 4 8 16 32 64 (double the number each time)*

1 4 9 16 25 36 (add 2 more each time)

1 2 4 7 11 16 22 29 37 (add 1 more each time)

0 1 1 2 3 5 8 13 21 34 (add the previous two numbers together)

P42:

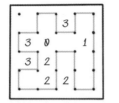

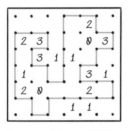

P43:
(left)

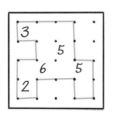

P43:
(right)

P45:

	6	5
8	5	3
3	1	2

	13	9
17	12	5
5	1	4

	23	19	12
23	9	11	3
21	9	6	6
10	5	2	3

	23	19	7
20	10	9	1
15	6	6	3
14	7	4	3

	4	24		
12	2	10	6	
10	2	5	3	17
	20	9	1	10
		9	2	7

ANSWERS

P46: The pentagon, diamond, and wide H tesselate.

P47: The pentagon and diamond tesselate.

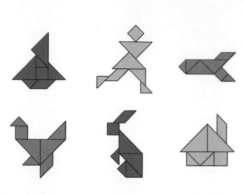

P55:

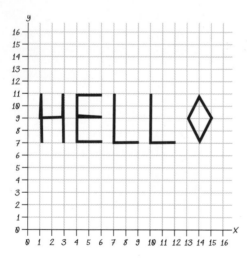

P57: The square has 38 triangles, the star has 34.

P59: 1b, 2d, 3c.

P80-81:

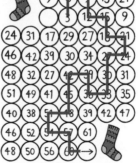